Urban Warrior

Biography of John Joseph George

A man on a mission from God

in Northwest Detroit

Kishell

Urban Warrior

ISBN:1500768286
ISBN-13:9781500768287

January 23, 2015

To the Northfield Twp Library

Making the Impossible Possible !

KIshell

Dedication

To God, my creator,

To the Holy Spirit, my inspiration,

To Jesus Christ my Savor.

In Honor of my Father

Joseph Stephen Kishel

August 7, 1914 – October 12, 2006

Published August 7, 2014
in Memorial of 100 years of his Spirit!

Kishell

Lynne Huff Kishell

Illustrations

NON-PROFIT

All proceeds from Urban Warrior support Motor City Blight Busters

Acknowledgments

Any creative work begins with an inspiration and in this case the voice of God. I must give thanks to Abba our Father for the first words, the message, the faith and the determination to see this project through. Praise and glory to our Almighty Creator.

This work of art took many hands to create. It began with John George who gave many hours and interviews to bring the story together. As with everything he does it was his passion and inspiration that fed the story. Truly his spirit lives within these pages.

To tell a personal story a writer knows that it takes the perspective of many to create the picture of a person — like any individual it too is multi-dimensional. It is the story of so many others that brought this canvas to life. It was a privilege to interview each of John's family and friends who were so open and eager to share their accounts of life with John.

Throughout the book the experiences shared by the volunteers and partners contributes to the heart and soul of the story. Memorializing, only the way that they could, the army of dedicated followers brought the stories close to home, sharing their own transformation and belief in making the impossible possible.

Thank you for giving your time and commitment to this dream and for sharing your story here.

To tell a story in front of a group, while uncomfortable at times, allows for a freedom to speak freely. To add emphasis and emotion where it is called for comes naturally. The flow can be adjusted to match the audience. There is some control the speaker has with delivery. Meanwhile, a manuscript begs for precise words that are chosen to speak the emotion, the thoughts must flow in a fashion that the reader can comprehend and follow. And with all this the grammar and text must follow the rules and order of the language. A writer may deliver the content but it is the editor that applies it to the canvas and creates what becomes the final piece of art.

I am indebted to Faith Doody who worked with me for over a year painstakingly making the edits, helping to create this beautiful work of art. Faith, as I, volunteered her time and talent to bring Urban Warrior to reality. She was not only professional, but considerate in her changes, always looking to keep the feel and message, only to enhance the story with richness and color. You are a blessing Faith thank you for all your dedication and helping to make this dream a reality!

"You can't tell a book by its cover", is often said, but if the cover doesn't grab you, you will never even read the book. Dave Budnick was the creative genius behind the cover of Urban Warrior. He is an amazing photographer with, not just an eye for the picture, but had the imagination to take it to the next level. His inspiration to have the marquee as the backdrop was perfect and told a story itself. Thank you Dave for creating a cover that calls out to capture the reader.

The cover wouldn't be possible without the support of the Motor City Organ Society Redford Theatre in particular Linda Sites who enthusiastically supported the idea and made the arrangements for this impromptu sign change for the photo shoot. Appreciation goes to Linda and her team for making this happen.

With any large undertaking, it requires the support of our loved ones. It is their encouragement and understanding when the tedious chore of the work takes over for other events and gatherings. My husband, Bill Huff, bless his soul, encouraged me for many years to continue this passionate venture. Following Bill's unexpected death I was at a loss and the inspiration took leave.

My daughters, Heather Bryant and Dana Livernois and my sisters Margaret (Pam) Tront and Mary (Hope) Johnson have given me encouragement, always believing in me. Their love has been a source of strength for me even when life seemed too hard and painful.

The last few months my life has been filled with hope and a new breath fills my soul. Jerry Puroll, my fiancé has brought me much happiness and joy and the encouragement I needed to pick up this important mission. Through his support I am able, with pen in hand, to sign my name to this final draft.

Introduction

A still, small voice. It was that still, small voice that spoke to me. That whisper of God that fills our hearts and minds. Often times it is lost in the noise of our lives. It is such a hush that we ignore it and continue in step with our routine. It takes a life-changing experience to allow that still, small voice to reach us. So it began when, suffering through a tumultuous dissolution of my employment and the losses associated with that, I began to hear that voice. I was going through a time of grieving and searching. I was taken to a new place in prayer and the Spirit of God was, not just reaching out to me, but working through me. Even though I recognized that voice, I was still set to ignore it, saying, "Oh no, not I, Lord." But our Lord persists. We can always choose to ignore that still, small voice. We can fill our lives with distractions, games, movies, music, recreation, exercise, and just move on with our lives.

But I did choose to hear that voice. A voice that led me back to my friend John George and the Motor City Blight Busters family. I had been volunteering with John and his bunch of blight fighters for over twelve years. As a youth minister with Christ the Redeemer Church in Lake Orion, Michigan, I would bring teens to Northwest Detroit to learn something about changing a community and how their small hands could make a world of difference. I knew in my heart that there was more to this mission of mine than just introducing the young people to this man with a passion for justice. I was called to share his vision and message with the world.

So, why is this book about John George and not, simply put, Motor City Blight Busters? Actually, I don't believe you can have one without the other, but the point of writing the biography of John George is to explore the man who is, as John likes to say, "the man behind the curtain," and how this man who is "larger than life" got that way.

Throughout all of time there have been those people who have stood out, people who faced the impossible head on, people who defied the odds and sacrificed their personal well-being for what they believed in. Right here in the City of Detroit many names and faces come to mind. There is Henry Ford, whose invention of the assembly line and eventually the $5 workday catapulted him into history and fame. In the music industry there is, of course, more than one person who can claim Motown fame, but leading the pack would be our own Stevie Wonder who was a mentor and inspiration for many others from Detroit. Wonder's ability to overcome blindness and become the only solo artist to have won twenty-two Grammy Awards makes him a Detroit legend. There's also Ernie Harwell, renowned for his sports-casting style and a man of grace, who after 42 years of serving as the sportscaster for the Detroit Tigers, ranked 16th on its list of Top 50 Sportscasters of All Time by the American Sportscasters Association. Charles Lindbergh, a Detroit native, was awarded the Medal of Honor in 1927 for displaying heroic courage and skill as a navigator, at the risk of his life, on his historic nonstop flight in the "Spirit of St. Louis," from New York City to Paris, France, 20–21 May 1927. (Charles Lindbergh Medal of Honor, 1998)

To that list we can add John Joseph George. He might not be known in Africa or Europe, in Maine or California, but to the people in the northwest corner of Detroit, he is a hero. He is a man who has created his own legacy. This is his story. And this is my attempt to answer the question: What makes one person dedicate his life to a single vision, sacrificing personal gain in order to change so many lives?

I hope in some way, you may hear that still, small voice and create your own vision to change lives.

Peace, my friends!

Kishell

No matter how dark it gets - if you quit and turn around, you are not going to know what is on the other side of that curtain.

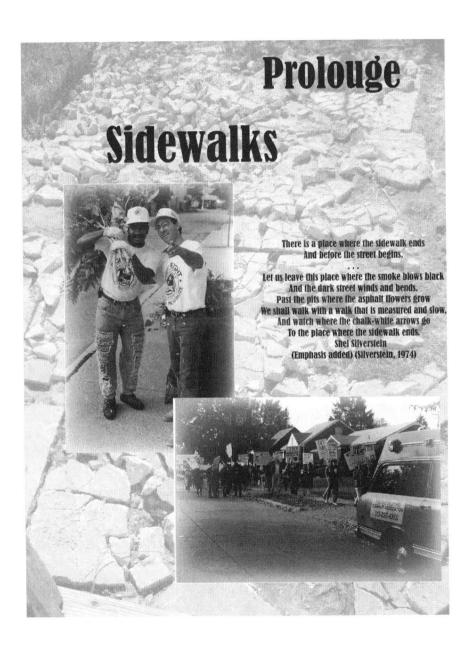

Prolouge

Sidewalks

There is a place where the sidewalk ends
And before the street begins,
...
Let us leave this place where the smoke blows black
And the dark street winds and bends.
Past the pits where the asphalt flowers grow
We shall walk with a walk that is measured and slow,
And watch where the chalk-white arrows go
To the place where the sidewalk ends.
Shel Silverstein
(Emphasis added) (Silverstein, 1974)

A story sometimes opens at the beginning of a life, sometimes at the end of a life; sometimes at a specific incident that an author focuses on to captivate the reader. This story begins not in the middle, the end or the beginning, nor with a specific incident. It begins with a spirit. A spirit found on the sidewalks of Old Redford, "the Village". A spirit that John Joseph George embraces, that spirit is at the heart of this story. And so we begin on the sidewalk . . .

"Hey Buddy" John sings out to the stranger as he leaves out of the café. "How's it goin' today?" The man looks on, in disbelief, then returns John's welcoming smile and greeting with "Good morning to you sir. A fine day." John shakes the man's hand and says, "Have a blessed day."

"John does not have a disingenuous bone in his body," his sister Diana Jacokes shares . "He has respect for every single person he encounters. He lives real close to the skin. He is just right there."

We jump into John's new, bright red 2012 VW, a gift from Oprah, and we are off. John is going to show me where he grew up.

We are on Detroit's northwest side that is made up of several small neighborhoods. The six-square mile neighborhood where John grew up is known as Brightmoor, situated alongside Old Redford, where John currently lives.

It is a sunny, warm fall day. Leaves blanket the ground with a carpet of gold, covering the weeds, debris and dirt of the streets here in Old Redford, as John begins the tour of his childhood neighborhood. The first stop on the tour is just blocks away from the Motor City Blight Busters headquarters, Redford High School. Once a gem of Detroit it proudly housed as many as 2,800 students at a time and graduated thousands of enthusiastic teens over its 81 years of operation. Now it stands as another abscess of a cancer that seems to have taken over this corner of the City.

John has a way of hypnotizing his listeners and before long they are taken away with him from a place of uncertainty, disappointment and despair to a world of possibility, excitement and energy! This is not just a man with a vision, but a man who can magically materialize that vision for everyone else to see. As John's voice lifts a notch with his excitement, a whole new scene seems to morph before his audience. The landscape miraculously changes to one of newly paved sidewalks filled with people flowing past beautiful trees and planters cascading with sprays of autumn flowers! Instead of a decaying edifice, the old high school is now a sprawling grocery store complex. John explains that this will not only provide the community with much-needed fresh and healthy food, but will also provide jobs for local workers.

It is estimated that as many as 83 full-time workers and 208 part-time employees will be employed here, an estimate given by the Michigan Economic Development Corporation (MEDC) board. Detroit is but one of many major cities facing the plight of being a food desert, that is, a place where the only food options for the community are gas stations, fast food havens and the occasional corner store. John continues to explain that Meijer has set its sights on this piece of property for one of its large grocery/shopping centers. As of this writing, Meijer was in negotiations with Detroit Public Schools and Michigan Economic Growth Authority (MEGA). MEGA approved tax breaks "for the Grand Rapids chain to build a retail and grocery store at the site of the former Redford High School. . . Meijer is considering investing $33 million to build a 217,000-square-foot store with a grocery, garden center and gas station at 21431 W. Grand River Avenue after the public-private MEGA board approved a $3.3 million tax credit and other state and local tax breaks."

(Trop, 2011)

As John starts the car rolling again, we drive around the block and he continues on to explain how Blight Busters is working with the MEDC to negotiate a contract to demolish the site. A little farther along the back of the lot, where the old ball fields existed, he explains that Blight Busters currently has a contract to remove the bleachers, which will bring in some income as scrap material. Around the corner, with those rose colored glasses in place again, he is describing how the beautiful old stone building, sitting on the corner, once home to the Redford Public Library, is being granted to Motor City Blight Busters through an agreement with Lomax Sterns, the developers of the site. The plan for how this historical landmark will be part of the new landscape is ever evolving. First there was a plan to create a day care center for the employees of the new super store. Next it was envisioned as a restaurant serving locally grown and prepared food that would not only provide more healthy choices for local residents, but would also continue the vision of building the neighborhood block by block while supporting each segment of the community.

We continue on this little road trip just a few blocks east to Chapel Street, north of Fenkell. Here is where John was born. We look at the first three houses from the corner, and John is not quite sure which is the house where he first lived. He lived in this location until he was just a year old and his memory is a little clouded. A call to his mother confirms that it was the third house. A beautiful new brick, single-story home sits on the lot and John continues to explain, with a chirp in his voice, "Yes, I remember this lot! My buddy, John O'Brien and I tore down the house that was located here. I guess, the one I grew up in. I didn't realize that at the time." O'Brien is the ex-Director of Northwest Detroit Neighborhood Development (NDND) and is a long-time friend of John's. O'Brien builds new homes on many of the vacant sites acquired through Blight Busters.

The Motor City Blight Buster's mission, "To stabilize, and revitalize the neighborhoods of Detroit, with a focus on Old Redford and adjacent communities, by utilizing targeted and coordinated revitalization efforts, including, home acquisitions, restoration and sale; new home construction and sale, demolition, neighborhood cleanup/beautification and education and skills training", is at the heart of everything that John does. As we proceed around a corner, John brings the car to a halt and jumps out, shouting back, "This is a friends house, I'll be right back." The door is open and John calls out to see if someone is home. When there is no response, he goes in and surveys the house inside and out, closes and locks the door behind him, and comes back to join me. He explains that his friend bought this house a short while back and has not moved in yet. Finding the door open and no one home, he secured the premises and we moved on.

This is John living the mission. Mission statements are creative and usually etched out by stakeholders in an organization after much thought, discussion, strategizing and deliberation. The Motor City Blight Busters mission statement is simply a verbal interpretation of what John has been living and breathing every day since he first boarded up a home for the sake of his community.

Let us segue into the Blight Buster's story here for a moment before we return to our car ride. Those who have never volunteered for Blight Busters or visited Artist Village Detroit you have not heard this story. But anyone who has stepped foot on the pavement near Lahser and Grand River has probably heard it more than once. The story is no secret, and John's mission includes educating everyone who passes through. He never seems to tire of telling "the story." He is like a vocalist who can sing the hit that made him famous over and over again, year after year, and make it fresh and alive as if he is singing it for the first time, each time. The audience falls into a trance as that song spills forth, mesmerized by John's energy and enthusiasm.

Usually standing on a porch, a pile of debris, or the top of a dumpster, wearing his uniform, the Blight Buster's shirt, The Detroit Tiger's baseball cap with the Old English D logo, black jeans and a beat-up pair of Nikes. John gathers everyone in and begins: "Thank you folks for all comin' out today to help Blight Busters remove some negative energy and create a positive, clean, green space for the community here in Old Redford!"

Next John expounds a little on the project perhaps giving a little background on the history and story behind the site. Usually it goes something like this: "This was a beautiful family home for many years, but because of bad times, it became abandoned and decay set in. More recently, those who wrap themselves in negative energy, drug dealers and criminals, came in and set up shop here. They threaten the neighbors' safety and the health of the children in the community. One thing leads to another and the house is firebombed. Perhaps it is a drug dealer seeking revenge; maybe someone in the community sets the blaze in an attempt to remove the problem and sometimes, the criminals themselves do it. The house is not just an eyesore, but becomes a danger to children in the area who might wander in and fall through a weak floor, or be bitten by a rat or other wild animal that has made a home amongst the charred remains." The story varies a little, but always seems to educate the volunteers on the term "negative energy".

Every organization has its own coined words and phrases, and "negative energy" is certainly one of the key phrases of Blight Busters. When John describes this plight of blight, day in and day out, these two words take on a very dark and complicated meaning. At the worksite, surrounded burnt remains, the negative energy is easily recognizable But, continued conversations with John will reveal that this negative energy describes much more; it is a sense of loss, hopelessness that not only lives beneath the surface of the rubble, but blows through the precarious structures, around the corner, through the streets and along the roads. It is what fuels the problem, eats at the youth, and creates a perpetual spiral of injustice. This is what John sees and feels everyday and is perhaps what feeds his passion. While John can deftly lead his listeners to appreciate the problem, he is careful to quickly move to the hope, the light and the positive energy that he is helping to grow. In fact, within minutes the volunteers are moved to become that light of hope, and are quick to pick up the tools that will help them transform this small space.

Before he moves on, John digs in one more time. "This is my home and my neighborhood," he explains. "I grew up just a few blocks west of here; now I live down the street. When I began this project 24 years ago, it was because I was sick and tired of what drug dealers were doing here. I was worried for my children's safety; and, just because the City was not going to do anything about it, I was not going to let that stop me from protecting my family." (George J. , John George Second Interview, 2011)

There was an abandoned house behind our home that had turned into a crack house. John William was two and Ann Marie hadn't even been born yet. Ann, my wife was pregnant with her. We called the Mayor, we called the police, we called the City, we called City Council we called everyone that we could call and no one would come. So every Thursday, Friday, and Saturday, these guys would set up shop and cause trouble and wouldn't move. I said, "Well, wait a minute. I pay my mortgage, I go to work, I pay my taxes, I take out my trash, I cut my grass and I spray the weeds out of my cracks (ha ha) so why do I gotta move? I'm not going to go anywhere."

That was kind of a gauntlet when I laid it down. I was doing everything I was supposed to do but the Mayor wouldn't fix it, the City wouldn't fix it, the City Council wouldn't fix it, the Office of Building and Safety wouldn't fix it, the Ombudsman's Office wouldn't fix it, the police officers won't fix it. Nobody would do anything. Obviously, they were busy. So I bought plywood and nails, and went back to the house and set up a workshop on the front lawn. I connected three extension cords from my garage for electricity. I marched down the street, plugged in my saw and started cutting the wood.

That's when Felix and Albert showed up, the other founding fathers of Blight Busters. We worked nine hours that day. We boarded up the house, we painted the boards, we cut the grass, we trimmed the bushes, we cleaned the cracks, rediscovered the sidewalk, put all the trash on the curb. When the drug dealers came back they couldn't get in, so they got back in their jeep and they left. That was simple. So that is what we have been doing ever since. (George J. , John George Second Interview, 2011.

We continue the trip down memory lane and stop at Vaughan and Eaton streets. Here sits a two-story gray brick home looking none the worse for fifty years of life and stories, John's childhood home. A couple of blocks down is St. Monica Catholic Church and School where John went to school and played ball with his friends in the back lot. He grew up in a time when the neighbors monitored the children from the front porch. It didn't matter if your mom or dad saw you, or what you were up to, because sure enough there was someone's parent down the street who knew what you were doing and would head right over to your house to inform your parents of your shenanigans. It was that kind of neighborhood and that kind of time. As John reminisced, "I could go down our block and tell you who lived where. It was like one big family. It is that sense of community, friendship, brotherly love, neighborhood, that I want to recreate.

A Tale of Two Cities
Old Redfored and Detroit

1

It was the best of times, it was the worst of times, it was the age of wisdom, it was the age of foolishness, it was the epoch of belief, it was the epoch of incredulity, it was the season of Light...

Charles Dickens: A Tale of Two Cities

"Old Redford is about a square mile and was incorporated in 1832. It was actually a part of a land grant, from the President at the time, Andrew Jackson, to the territory of Michigan. There were a lot of farmhouses built around that time. Matter of fact, the house where I live now is 100 years old; it was built in 1913. I have all the paperwork and the deed. The house next to my house, was the original farmhouse of Mr. Woolworth. He had 80 acres, which was probably where we are sitting. (At the Java House, on Lahser at Grand River) Matter of fact, his farmhouse burned down and I ended up tearing it down and demolishing it. There is now a new home that we built on that site in 2001." (George J. , John George Second Interview, 2011)

BRIGHTMOOR

The winds blow across vacant lots and through overgrown weeds and debris; they whip the papers across the yards of abandoned structures that once were homes for families. In Brightmoor, many of these little clapboard houses were built in the late 20's and early 30's to accommodate the veterans returning from World War I along with the young people coming up from the South to secure the five-dollar-a-day jobs being offered by Henry Ford. Built away from the hustle and bustle of the downtown world those homes were a quick fix to the growth problem, a cluster of family homes where workers could live within reasonable distance from the factories located in Dearborn and Detroit.

From 1920 to 1925 the population in Detroit increased percent, expanding out into the farmland. (Martelle) The area that became known as Brightmoor was located five miles northwest of the city. "Bounded on the south by the Pere Marquette Railroad, and on the west by Telegraph Road, the east to Woodward, and to the North side by a jagged line, from Kentfield to Bentler Avenue and north to Puritan Avenue, . . . Roughly, an area of about 14 square miles this flat land was well suited for development." (Detroit Bureau of Governmental Research and the School of Public Affairs and Social Work of Wayne University Report No. 19, 1940). The plight of Brightmoor has its roots in this rush to create neighborhoods without the planning. There were no zoning laws, no infrastructure, no plan whatsoever. Simply put, tracts of farmland were sold off in plots for the new owners to do as they pleased. And so they did. (George A. M., 2011)

Families anticipating exciting new opportunities and built their homes. They soon discovered that the lack of basic services, water, roads, fire protection and schools weren't included in the package.   Many of the new families struggled along, while others were able to move on to the new suburbs being built with more thought and planning. Those who stayed made the best of their situation and, with a little help from the city and federal governments the infrastructure gradually filled in around them.

The decades, passed and in the 1960s the riots changed the demographics once again. The joy and hope that had filled the playgrounds, streets and local businesses in the few years of contentment were now replaced with fear, suspicion, anger and uncertainty. Houses that had been built with so much hope and promise for a new beginning, were giving way to age due to their poor construction. Shingles loosened, siding peeled away, sidewalks cracked; time passed on and over the fences.   The families who remained were struggling.   The homeowners who had once been prospering autoworkers were now elderly and living on a limited income.   Younger homeowners included many who had fallen on hard times and were struggling to make ends meet.

Then came the '70s and '80s, the homes devalued even more, seemingly overnight, they were taken over by banks and transferred into HUD homes. The decades moved on and these little houses deteriorated further: walls cracked, roofs leaked giving way to mold, ceiling decay, rot, and collapse. Families abandoned the houses, the grass grew into weeds, and the shrubbery that once adorned the yards now engulfed the houses, climbing through the windows.

With the '90s a new type of family moved in. Within the shadows of night, cloaked in their own darkness, the homeless, rats, drug dealers and prostitutes became the newest residents. In one single block there might be a 90-year-old original homeowner living next door to a crack house, next door to that might be a single mother on welfare trying to raise her two children and next to that yet another drug house. Through this struggle the turmoil brewed. Drug dealers fought for their territory, neighbors fought the drug dealers, and houses burned. Then came John George, a man with a mission.

~

OLD REFORD

Old Redford sits just north of the Brightmoor neighborhood. Old Sand Hill, as it was originally referred to because of the sandy ridge where the first houses were built, sits along Grand River Avenue. The Village grew out of the 100 acres purchased by homesteader Solomon Burt in 1820. A school was built in 1837, and by the 1890s there were about 100 people living in Sand Hill, which had become a stop on the Detroit United Electric Railway. In 1906, Sand Hill was combined with Redford Village, a name that evolved from the Rouge River. Rouge is the French word for red, the name given to the river because of its natural red clay bed. The river passes through the township and was even used as a mode of travel during the early years before Old Blank Road (later named Grand River) was built. There was a ford in the river, a shallow that could be crossed by foot. Rouge became "red" and combined with "ford" to create the name Redford.

Redford became a thriving community of affluence. A theatre was built in 1928 to accommodate the growing cultural interests of the residents. It was billed as "America's Most Unique Suburban Playhouse." The three-story structure, with its grand entrance, was a jewel that drew crowds from all over the city to enjoy not only movies, but also large-scale presentations and events. Boasting a Baron Theatre Organ to accommodate the silent films of the time, it was a premier venue. The interior design was influenced by the owner's wife, who had recently traveled to Japan and came back with the idea to use Japanese art décor as the design motif for the theatre. When the Japanese attacked Pearl Harbor in 1941 the walls were quickly covered with a beige paint. The Old Redford Theatre is today known as the Motor City Organ Society

Redford Theatre.

This beloved landmark has survived through difficult financial times due to the diligence of the Motor City Organ Society, which has maintained and refurbished the grand theatre through the past several decades. Its efforts have not only helped saved the grand theatre, but have influenced the business becoming an anchor for this crumbling four corner village.

~

A TALE OF TWO CITIES

Brightmoor and Old Redford were two unique communities growing side by side out of the virgin farmlands of history, two cities growing in different directions. It was into this world that John Joseph George was born. With one foot in Brightmoor and the other in Old Redford, John celebrates the rich heritage of this land that sits at the ford of the Rouge River. Out of this small corner of Northwest Detroit, John George a man with passion and vision would transform these two communities from the ravages of time and decay, into communities where dreams are cultivated into reality and the future is making the impossible possible.

His Name Is John Big Bad John   2

Through the dust and smoke of this man-made hell Walked a giant of a man that the miners knoew well. Grabbed a saggin' timber, gave out with a groad and like a giant oak tree he just sood there alone - Big John, Big Bad John.

Jimmy Dean - Big John

June 24, 1958, it was a pleasant summer night on the corner of Trumbull and Michigan Avenue in Detroit. Paul Foytack was pitching in Briggs Stadium and the crowd was charged as the last run came in and the Detroit Tigers shut out the Baltimore Orioles in a 5-0 game. Meanwhile, just a few blocks away at Memorial Hospital, (previously St. Mary's) John Joseph George took his first breath, cradled in the arms of his mother Virginia as Edmund Francis, looked down at his beautiful new son.

The account of John Joseph George's life must begin a little further back in time. With a little bit of genealogy to set the stage for the entrance of this newest member of the George family who would one day change the world, "starting with Detroit." Edmund Francis George born in Detroit to parents of Lebanese decent, Salem and Minerva grew up in the southwest corner of Detroit not far from Virginia Conflitti, who was also a native Detroiter growing up in the Holy Redeemer Parish neighborhood of Livernois and Junction on Toledo Street. But it wasn't until 1946 that the two would meet.

World War II had come to a close and Edmund had returned home from his tour of duty in France. It was time for him to enjoy life, and what better way than to laugh, sing and dance? Ballrooms were popular spots for entertainment then, and Detroit boosted several renowned dance floors that heralded the big band sounds of Tommy Dorsey, Glenn Miller and Benny Goodman. The Graystone on Woodward and Canfield was just such a hall and "Wednesday night was Catholic night. All the kids from Catholic schools would go just that one night a week. That is where I met Edmund." Virginia shares. (George V. , 2012)

For Edmund it was love at first sight. Carol Kirkland, John's second oldest sister, recalls the story her mother would tell. "The first night they met, my dad said, 'I'm going to marry you.' My mother said 'You're crazy." He said, 'No, I'm not,'" and asked for her phone number. So he called her to go out on the second date and she said, 'I don't do that. I don't go out on the first phone call.' So he hung up and called her right back and said, 'Okay, this is the second call will you go out with me?' That next date was to the Vanity Ballroom and the beginning of many happy years together." (Kirkland C. , 2012)

Edmund and Virginia were married on September 16, 1948 at Holy Redeemer Catholic Church, where Virginia had been baptized, and made her First Communion and Confirmation. With a new job and little savings, the couple began their married life sharing space in the home of Virginia's parents, Maria and Dominic Conflitti, on Logan

Street. The babies soon followed. Diana was the first born on August 24, 1949, followed quickly by Carol Ann on July 15, 1950, and then Edmund Michael on December 23, 1951. With space in the house at a premium it was time to find a home of their own. Edmund's work at Ford Motors Company provided a modest but steady income, and in 1952 they were able to purchase their first home on Chapel Street on Detroit's northwest side in the Brightmoor neighborhood. A year later Robert Salem joined the family on August 31, 1953, and a few years later John came along to make a family of seven.

The family had quickly outgrown their little bungalow, and in October of 1959 the Georges moved to their permanent family home, just a couple of blocks over on the corner of Vaughan and Eaton. It was a beautiful brick home with an upstairs, basement and a garage, providing plenty of room for their growing family. Here, the last member of the George family was born, Michael Dominic, on September 12, 1960 making their family complete.

It was a time of recovery and progress for the country and the world. Times were a little slower and simpler. Most families were fortunate if they owned a car. And, while the country was in the grip of a recession, mothers were still the center of home life and the fathers were the breadwinners. A neighborhood was not a community, but rather a family. Doors were left unlocked and might show up in the living room. Virginia George recalls, coming down from upstairs one day. "There was Fr. Divine, our pastor at St. Monica's, sitting on the couch, watching the television!" (George V. , 2012)

That was life in the late '50s. There was an innocent trust that came with living in such a neighborhood and time. Children spent most of their waking hours outdoors, and respected their friends' moms and dads, who would not hesitate to correct them if they stepped out of line. It was just the way it was. "There must have been ninety kids in our neighborhood," Virginia ponders as she tallies off the families. "There were seven children in the Diroth family, eight in the Harmon family, nine in the Kelly family, eight in the Daniels family," and the list continued. (George V. , 2012)

The door to the George home was always open, and people young and old would stream in and out through out the day. If they weren't friends of John or one his five siblings, they were cousins or any one of the many neighbors that happened upon their doorstep. All were welcome here. It was this atmosphere that shaped John's sense of community, seeing not neighbors, not acquaintances but family. Everyone was family.

The George family was a humble one, living frugally on one income and budgeting so each child would have a parochial school education. They attended St. Monica and St. Christine elementary schools, later followed by Catholic high schools. About the time that John was born, Edmund made a career change to pursue a private insurance practice. As fate would have it, the recession seemed to hit just as he left Ford Motor Company making a frugal living even more challenging. Things may have been tight, but the children never seemed to notice. There was always food on the table and an abundance of love and happiness.

The George family's typical "summer vacation" was a testimony to their frugal lifestyle. With the construction of interstates and a network of roads across the country there was a surge of families that were loading up their cars and traveling miles upon miles to visit historical sights. That was not to be for the Georges; they had their own version of the family vacation. According to John's sister Carol, "I remember Dad saying that his idea of a vacation wasn't piling six kids into a station wagon and traveling anywhere, when he could just be in his backyard having a barbeque and swimming in his pool. So that's what we did, and there were people at the house constantly." (Kirkland C. A., 2012)

If the kitchen was the center of the world for Mrs. George, the backyard and barbeque defined Mr. George's world.

This is where he felt like a king entertaining his family, neighbors, friends and all wondered into his domain. His specialty was shish kabobs, grilled to perfection as only a Lebanese native could. Here was a man who loved to entertain, a vivacious man full of laughter and attitude, who could keep a party going. And a festive gathering was what he enjoyed, whether it be the family and a few neighbors around the backyard barbeque or an all out bash. Life was meant to be celebrated birthdays, holidays, baptisms, first communions, and with six children there were lots of opportunities to celebrate.

Back then John and his brothers and sisters spent many days visiting Grandma and Grandpa Conflitti a few blocks down on Rockdale. Summer vacation there was like a camp outing on the lush city lot lovingly groomed by these Italian immigrants. Grandpa Conflitti had made this his little bit of Italy, with a garden that was only rivaled by the Garden of Eden. John sister Carol remembers, "There was an apricot tree, an apple tree, a peach tree, a plum tree, a mulberry bush that covered a gazebo, and they grew every vegetable, squash, eggplant, cabbage, tomatoes, peppers. You name it, they grew it." And there, beside the gazebo, the George children would pitch their tent and play through the day and night, having fun as only children can. Grandma would bring out sandwiches and a picnic would ensue. This special intergenerational time was made even more special when it involved helping Grandma can the harvest from the garden; making spaghetti sauce from the fresh tomatoes followed by rolling out the dough to make the spaghetti and ravioli pasta.   (Kirkland C. A., 2012)

And, of course, there was the family pet to add a source of entertainment. Virginia George shares, "One day this dog went walking past our gate and the kids let him come in the yard and it just kept coming back. We knew who the owner was so, I said, 'John, you better take the dog back.' Then the fellow said, 'We're moving, if you want the dog, you can have the dog'. And that's how we got the dog. My daughter Diana named "him" Cornelius, Jeremy Peabody, but we called her Corky. She had 45 puppies!" (George V. , 2012)

In the 1960s, like most children of the time, John enjoyed riding bikes, playing ball and finding fun in his own backyard. With a steady flow of kids through the house and yard John was never without an audience. He was a young version of Monty Hall, always hosting some type of event for the kids in the neighborhood, a Millionaires Party with a real spinning wheel that he fashioned out of some castoffs, a homemade miniature golf course, and then there was the go-kart. "When we moved to Vaughan, he wanted to buy a go-kart from one of the boys down the street," recalls his sister Carol. "I think it was $3 or $5, which was a lot of money for him back then. It was the kind that you would steer with a rope tied to the wheels and someone would push you. He told the boy selling it, 'I will get you the money; just let me give people rides on it until I can pay for it.' So for a nickel he would take people around the block until he got enough money to buy the go-kart. (Kirkland C. A., 2012)

As the family grew and blossomed, so did the insurance business that Edmund had nurtured just as he did his family. His charisma and leadership were qualities key to grooming the business into a thriving enterprise, a business that provided the much-needed income to support the continuing education of his children.

In the fall of 1976, John enrolled in the Culinary Arts Program at Henry Ford Community College. Working at Maple House as a cook, John wanted to turn his love of cooking into a career. Taking the rudimentary general requirements along with the cooking courses, John was quick to find that college wasn't quite meant for him. It was his accounting instructor who set him straight. "I took some college classes in culinary arts, but as we all know I am no accountant it was my accounting instructor who made that clear. I was failing miserably in accounting and one day, I was late for class and Professor Brandt said; 'John George come here.' He looked at me and said; 'You're always late.' I said; 'That's true, I don't care for this class too much.' He said, 'Well I don't care for you too much either.   How would you like to get a "C" in accounting?' I said, 'That would be great because I'm failing so what do I have to do?' And he said; 'Never show your face in the accounting wing again!' And that's how I got the "C" in accounting!

It is here, in the fall of 1977, that life changed for John and his family. They were forever transformed by the death of their father and husband, Edmund, who was taken from them far too soon. A reality that Edmund himself knew all too well.

John remembers Edmund telling the story of his own father's sudden and unexpected death. Edmund George, his sister Charlotte and brother Eddie were being raised by their father after their mother had died, at the time of the story Edmund was about ten. John explain;

> *My dad, then about nine or ten years old, had been asleep and woke up when his father came in and said, "Wake up! Wake up! What is wrong?" "Oh my God, Dad, I had this terrible dream. I was sleeping and when I got up I was walking down the steps, the Lone Ranger Show was on the radio. The doorbell rang and there was this little old lady in a black dress and she said "Is your name Edmund George? Is your father's name Salem George?" He said, "Yes", "I hate to tell you, but he was just killed in a car crash." He broke out crying and his dad said "I am right here, obviously, so get up."*

As the story goes, in the dream it had been an early Saturday morning. So my dad would make sure that every Saturday morning he would get up and get out of bed before the Lone Ranger came on. One Saturday he woke up late. He was walking down the steps, the Lone Ranger was on the radio and there was a knock at the door. He went to the door and that lady was there, and she said, "Is your name Edmund Francis George? Your father Salem George was killed in an automobile accident." His father had been crossing the street with his younger brother, Eddie, when a car almost hit Eddie. I guess he went to push his brother out of the way to save him, and the car hit him instead.

Edmund and his siblings, homeless and orphaned, went to live with their Uncle Joe and Aunt Veronica. One can only imagine their grief and deep sense of loss. Perhaps this was the moment when Edmund took his grief and transformed it into lightheartedness, a way to cope with the senseless tragedy. Edmund is remembered by everyone as a gregarious man, a man with "a great sense of humor, a great laugh, loved by everyone that knew him a man with a really great heart." Carol shares. This was a man full of life, called home by God to early. (Kirkland C. , 2012)

Edmund's health had taken a turn in 1976 when he suffered a heart attack and underwent mitral valve surgery. Back then, the surgery required a median sternotomy - an incision through the midline of the sternum - a procedure so invasive that the ribcage had to be sawed in order to access the arteries.

Edmund's recovery was slow, requiring a stay of three months in the hospital.   Nine months later, the first week of September, 1977, the family had just gathered to celebrate the Labor Day holiday. John's sister Carol recalls, "I remember sitting with him at the kitchen table that weekend. It was just the two of us and he said, 'You know what Carol, I am sick and tired of being sick and tired.' The next morning he suffered the second heart attack that he never recovered from."   (Kirkland C. , 2012)

People gathered from near and far to send off this soul so full of love, laughter and good will. John remembers their neighbor, Mrs. Harman, reflecting on Edmund dying of an enlarged heart; "of course he did, because he had a big heart."

As Edmund George was laid to rest the lives of the remaining George family were about to change. The family insurance business, up to this point, had been run by John's mother, Virginia George, Edmund George, Jr. and, Edmund George senior, a thriving business as it was, required a lot to keep it going. John and Robert, the youngest of the George siblings, stepped in to take some of the critical pieces, helping keep the family business going and prospering. John put on a suit and tie and became a salesman in the family business. Making calls and networking with people came easily enough but sitting behind a desk and doing paperwork was never something that he adapted to.

It was during this time when John not only grew the business but, increased his own financial state to one that was quite handsome. The income afforded him a few luxuries that perhaps others would never be drawn to. While John enjoyed playing golf with his friends and professional associates, it was organizing parties that really energized him. It was as if this hobby was the balance he needed to maintain the career life that was so taxing to his soul. John's party performances put him in contact with many beautiful women and it was here that he met Ann Alexander the women he would marry and who would be beside him as he migrated to his next passion. Ann remembers fondly the night her sister's friend invited her to go to the club. "John was like a promoter he did a lot of parties. I went to a party with a friend of my sister's and she introduced us and I was just really taken by the fact that he was really popular and how many people knew him." (Interview, 2012)

Like his father John was smitten at that first dance and in a short time was married to Ann. It wasn't long and they had purchased their first home, the home that John would one day run his business from. The only thing needed to make this family complete was the addition of children and they indeed quickly follow. John William was born in November 26, 1986 followed by Ann Marie born August 26, 1988.

Are They For Real 3 or Just Crazy

Through the dust and the smoke
Of this man-made hell
Walked a giant of a man that the
miners knew well
Grabbed a saggin' timber,
gave out with a groan
And like a giant oak tree
he just stood there alone-
Big JohnBig Bad John

Jimmy Dean; Big John

In 1988, moved by his concern for his family, friends, neighborhood and city, John took action.

The two story brick house sits on a well-groomed corner lot of Lahser. This is where John has lived for the past twenty-five years. The second story is set-off with a beautiful balcony enclosed in a wood frame of windows that overlook a backyard boasting huge oak trees and beautiful 30-foot pines. Sitting in the enclosed porch off of the second floor of this one hundred year old home John reflects;

> *This is where it all started literally, looking out this back porch, 26 years ago. See that vacant lot on the other side of the street there, at the end of the block? That is where the famous crack house stood that we couldn't get rid of, on the 18000 block of Greydale. There were three major problems: that crack house, an abandoned fire-damaged house behind my garage, and there was a hoarder's special. The owner of the house was a pack rat extraordinaire. It literally took ten 40-yard dumpsters to remove everything from these three sites.*
>
> *It did take time, but little by little the view from this back window was filled with open lawns, a garden and beautiful trees. Ultimately, the crack house and abandoned firebombed house were torn down, and the third property was rehabbed. This three-story, five-bedroom house that had been the worst house in the neighborhood - after $45,000 of renovations - is the nicest. We literally touched every square inch, inside and out - central air, windows, new heating, new plumbing, new electrical.* (George J. J., How it all Got Started, 2012)

Small steps. It all began with those first, small steps of just reaching out and helping a neighbor. Two of those neighbors were Felix Wright and Albert E. Mack. Albert tells the story with a smile as he recalls his first encounter with John. Albert had bought the house next to his friend Felix, planning to move there in a few months once he had a chance to fix the place up. The adjoining empty lot that sat between his house and Felix's was a mass of weeds and vegetation that had grown out of control with the spring rain and early summer heat. Albert drove up to his property one Saturday, prepared to take on the task of cutting down the overgrowth and cleaning up the lot, but was shocked to find it all groomed. Turning to Felix, Albert asked if he had worked on the lot. With a chuckle he recalls Felix's response: "This guy came around the corner with this tractor and just cut the field down." I asked Felix, 'How much did he charge you?' and he said, 'Nothing, but his name is John.'"

About three months later, Mack moved into his house. He recalls, "John, Felix and the other men in the neighborhood all came out on Saturday mornings with their brooms and rakes and started sweeping the streets." While Albert admired the hard work and efforts of the men, he was a single father working the night shift, so Saturday mornings were his time to spend on the sofa with his kids watching cartoons. But that quickly changed with John and Felix's insistence that he come out and join the other men. From sweeping and cleaning the streets, they turned to closing up drug houses. "People would ask us, 'Do you work for the City? Do you work for the State?' 'NO!' 'Is someone paying you for this?' 'NO!' 'Then, why are you doing it?' We believed that we were on a mission from God. We really believed that. We felt that if we were on a mission from God, then nothing and no one could stop us, we could go into places nobody else would dare to go." And this was the beginning, not only of a long friendship, but a partnership that would build a successful nonprofit organization from a grassroots mission to save a neighborhood. (Mack, 2011)

During these early years, John worked as an insurance agent in his family's business with his brother Ed and his mother. He would do his cleanup work on weekends and after work hours. As time went on, his passion took him out of the office more and more, and into the streets or to meetings to gather resources and support.

One of these first meetings was with the Old Redford Business Association. John arrived at the monthly board meeting open minded and ready to gather some real support, but was sadly disappointed. "I went to the Association to see if I could get help to board up a house.

So I go to the meeting, and I sit down and I'm listening, and they have all these maps and charts, and they're saying 'We are going to do this and we are going to do that.' I respond, 'So, where are your rakes and brooms and shovels?' They answer, 'Oh, we don't have any of those.' I said, 'Wait a minute; you're the Old Redford Business Association, right? You guys are talking about the business district and neighborhoods, so why don't we coordinate some kind of cleanup effort?' Everyone just looked at me like I was nuts."

It seemed that apathy had set in. The Association and the people of the community had come to expect the City to take care of the problem. Meanwhile, the City steeped in its own financial and political woes wasn't interested in getting involved in a specific community's problem. Instead, it was trying to focus on the larger picture, promoting the City and bringing more business to the downtown area.

So John moved on, putting the Association and the apathy behind him, and creating the Old Redford Cleanup Association to meet the challenge head on. In the beginning, it was just the three of them: John, Albert and Felix. They would knock on doors and try to recruit whomever they could, but most times it ended up just being John himself who would walk up and down the streets, sweeping, picking up trash, cutting grass and doing whatever needed to be done.

It is often said, timing is everything and so it was with the launching of Blight Busters. God has a way of bringing the right people together at the right time and supplying everything that is needed when His work is being done. The picture began to come together one Saturday afternoon.

One Saturday, I was sitting on my porch after we had worked all day. I was exhausted. I was trying to get enough energy to just get up and go into the house so I could get cleaned up and get something to eat before I passed out. These two guys were walking down the street in their black pants, white shirts, and black ties - two white guys. I look at them and said, "Hey man, what are you doing?" So they came up and said, "Oh, we're known as the elders, we're from the Church of Jesus Christ of Latter Day Saints and we've been sent to preach." I said, "Okay." So we talked for a bit, sharing our views on religion. As they were getting ready to go, I said, "It was nice talking with you guys, be careful, and good luck." Walking away, one of them said, "Oh, and by the way, we also do community service." I said, "What? What did you say? Get back over here". "We also do community service." "What are you talking about?"

I explained to them that on Saturdays we got together with about 12 neighborhood folks to do community service right here. I said, "What are you doing next Saturday? "

So sure enough the next Saturday, 12 of these guys show up, the elders from the Church of Jesus Christ of the Latter Day Saints! They ended up being our first volunteer group. Now we had a bit of a force, where before it was just this one crazy white guy and two neighbors. There was a movement now!

Creating change requires resources, volunteers and a vision. John now had the volunteer base, all he needed were a few resources. Up to this point, he had been working out of his garage, using his own equipment: lawnmower, weed whacker, shovels, rakes and brooms. He was supplying garbage bags, gloves and all the miscellaneous items from his own pocket. Needless to say, he was going through lots of equipment and supplies not to mention the money, investing, on the average about $15,000 a year.

Shortly, after meeting up with the elders, John received an interesting phone call. Things were picking up as John's mission became more of a working business plan. As he used projects to leverage the media, the word was getting out and more people were hearing about the work he was doing in Northwest Detroit. One such person was Betty DeRamus, a highly acclaimed journalist and former columnist for the *Detroit News*, who wrote an article on the Old Redford Cleanup Association. As Providence would have it, a man on vacation in the Bahamas was reading the Detroit News when he came upon the story. This man was Dick Headlee, President of Morbark Industries and a member of the Alexander Hamilton Life Insurance Company Board of Directors. Headlee was a renowned politian best known for his design of the "Headlee Amendment." (Among its many provisions, it intended to limit government and protect taxpayers.) In 1982, he was the Republican nominee for governor of the State of Michigan. Headlee had another esteemed title though, that of Bishop and Regional Representative of the Church of Jesus Christ of Latter-Day Saints in Michigan. Perhaps it was Providence in more ways than one that would bring this man into partnership with John.

After reading the article, Mr. Headlee knew the person to call upon to investigate this whole interesting situation was, Jim Cope. Mr. Cope worked at Alexander Hamilton Life Insurance, and Mr. Headlee knew that Cope's parents lived in the Old Redford neighborhood about which Ms. DeRamus had written. As John recalls, Mr. Headlee made a phone call to Jim and said, "I'm reading the newspaper and there is this guy, John George, and he is down there in your mom and dad's neighborhood. Go down there and see if he is crazy, or if he is really doing something." Jim immediately called John and opened with, "Hey, John this is Jim Cope from Alexander Hamilton Insurance, my boss asked me to come out and see what you are doing over there in Brightmoor." That day, Jim did come out and meet with John, and a new partnership was formed.

The meeting began with John taking Cope on a tour of the neighborhood, showing him the project sites where work had been done, and the places where plans were in progress to remove more blight.

So sure enough Jim shows up and says, "My boss sent me out to see if you guys are for real, or if you're crazy!" So I took him through the neighborhood and showed him the first house that we boarded up, and I told him what we were doing and why we were doing it. At the end of the tour, Jim said, "So what do you need?" I said, "Man, we could use a couple lawnmowers, a chainsaw, some weed-whackers, rakes and brooms. We could use some work gloves and garbage bags anything you could help us with so we could clean up the neighborhood. That would be great." He says, "Alright!" Jim went back and talked to Mr. Headlee who gave the go ahead. The next weekend, Jim came back with a truck loaded up with it all!

Now John had the volunteers, the resources and a vision to stop the spread of blight! The following Tuesday was the Fourth of July and John was spending the day with family and friends in his backyard, with a good old-fashioned barbeque. It was there that the name for John's new organization was born. In his enthusiasm for his new acquisition of resources, John invited his friends to take a look at the stash. One of the guys grabbed the weed whacker, and swinging it around, he said, "Hey, these guys are like the *Ghostbusters!*" At that moment a light went off in John's head and he thought, "Hey, Blight Busters, that's what we are!"

All the puzzle pieces came together the following Saturday. The elders arrived on schedule, the tools and supplies were brought out, and Channels 2, 4 and 7 along with the *Detroit Free Press* and the *Chronicle* came out to cover the cleanup project on Orchard Street. When asked, "What do you call yourselves?" John shouted out with pride, "We're the Blight Busters!" The message went out through the community and the airwaves and John's movement took on a new look and a whole new energy.

Every movement needs an identity, a name, a logo and a mascot or symbol. John had the name Blight Busters and the logo quickly evolved out of the *Ghostbusters* theme. It was natural to think of a house and then add the universal symbol for "no" – a red circle with a line through it - to the picture. Albert shares that the colors of black and white were not chosen by accident; but were intentional in their effort to convey a sense of solidarity and unity. Albert felt the colors were a way to "celebrate that people of different ethnicities can come together and clean their city." Their symbol was a vintage, powder blue, International Harvester ambulance! John fondly recalls,

"One day I was driving down Telegraph, and there it was this powder blue ambulance going south. It took me a minute, but I was able to raise the money and the next thing I knew, we had the Blight Busters moving billboard."

The partnership with Mr. Headlee and the Alexander Hamilton Life Insurance group did much more than provide tools and financial support. It provided some of the administrative support that was needed to move the organization from a grassroots project to a legitimate nonprofit business. Just after their successful event in July of 1988, Jim Cope and a very committed group of volunteers from Alexander Hamilton known as, Hamilton Employees Love People, H.E.L.P provided the professional services needed to facilitate process for the organization to attain the 501 (c) (3) status that it needed to become an official not-for-profit business.

The Old Redford Cleanup Association had officially become Motor City Blight Busters, Inc. - and a movement to revitalize Northwest Detroit was launched, a movement that could not be stopped! The newly formed organization had mobilized, and with a presence in the Village, in the neighborhoods and on the street, they just needed a place to call home. That place would be the Masonic Temple, built in 1923 to house the growing Mason organization. The Mason's had begun "through the sentiments expressed by the returning soldiers during the early years of the Civil War". With an initial membership of twelve there were established on December 18, 1863;[i] by 1929 it had surged to a roll of 569 members. The four-story building on

Lahser Road, was the pride, not only of the Masons, but of the community as well, with its elegant third-floor theatre serving as an entertainment venue. The Mason Lodge was a cornerstone of the community for many years, until membership declined and the building fell into disrepair. In order to maintain the facility, the surrounding land was sold off piece by piece. Finally, the site was put on the market and sold to the State of Michigan, housing a division of the Department of Transportation for a period of time. (Company, Anniversary Souvenir, CH Krugler & Company)

What transpired after that is a little less clear, but it is John's recollection that it "was purchased by a young man who ran a church" out of the building. the Old Redford Business Association purchased it next, and then lost to the State for back taxes ." After that it was abandoned for some years.

The building that had been a gem for the early community - with oak floors, a winding staircase and beauty characteristic of early twenties architecture - had now become a home for pigeons and rats. A tenement for the dregs of the city, the homeless and the varmints. Windows were shattered, the roof leaked and what remained was damaged by the weather, if not by those who stripped it of any material value. The City condemned the building and it awaited demolition. It was in this darkness that a light shone. It was early July and the newly formed Blight Buster organization had just finished the momentous project on Orchard Street, when the next step of the journey began to unfold. (Company)

At the end of the day we were packing up and Felix looked over at the building (Masonic Lodge) and said, "I wonder if we can get that for our headquarter's?" That's where the whole idea came from. It wasn't even my idea; it was Felix's idea. I looked at him and said, " Of course we can!" (George J. J., Early Days Continuation, 2011)

It was the early 90's when John, with his best friend, Todd McKler, took the first interior inspection of the building. Standing just outside the structure, Todd said, "Are you crazy? Really, man, are you crazy?" They stepped through the darkness, knowing they were walking over debris embedded with not just rat feces, but human feces as well. With only a Bic lighter illuminating their path, they tried to negotiate the fallen beams and garbage. The hole was filled with discarded mattresses that were beds for the homeless and a resource for prostitutes. They could only hold their breath for so long before the putrid smell of urine and decomposition would fill their lungs. "Man, you are really crazy," Todd said to John as they negotiated their way through the old Masonic Lodge. (McKler, 2012)

This cavernous hole that seemed to be an opening to hell would take "five years, 1.4 million dollars and almost kill us", (George J. J., How it all Got Started, 2012) before becoming the headquarters for the Motor City Blight Busters. "I just built it. It has been quite an adventure."

John worked assiduously toward making his dream a reality. By 1995, it wasn't hard to notice the impact that John Joseph George and the Motor City Blight Busters were making on the community and the City.

"Saving the World

starting with Detroit."

4

VISIONARY

Just once in his life
A man has his time
And my time is now
And I'm comin' alive

I can hear the music playin'
I can see the banners fly
Feel like you're back again
And hope ridin' high
Gonna be your man in motion
All I need is a pair of wheels
Take me where my future's lyin'
St. Elmo's Fire

Maybe John's passion is fueled by his desire to make use of everything around him. Perhaps his identity as a "visionary" comes less from the philosophical interpretation of the word and more from the literal interpretation. John takes that old adage, "the whole is greater than the sum of the parts" very literally, creating something amazing from what others might see as simply junk.

"When he was little he was always working a deal," says his sister Diana Jacokes, "working an angle. On garbage day he would go around to the neighbors trash and pull out things that looked useful, and bring them back to our house and set up a flea market. He would then charge the neighbor kids to buy back their old stuff. One time he fashioned a go-kart out of some old stroller wheels. He charged the kids a quarter to push it around the block. It didn't have any real locomotion, you could only push it around but it would cost you money. And then he would do a millionaires party in our garage where kids would come and play black jack. It would cost them to play but then they would win a prize that he would fish out of the garbage!"

An angle, working a deal . . . maybe. But then again, John had a talent for taking junk and making it look like something more. In his own words, " I have always known how to fix things. I don't know how or why I know, I just know. Like taking things apart and putting things back together." He could take the insignificant and give it value. That is a gift and an art. Some call him a salesman. However, as John's story unfolds turning the insignificant into something of value became much more than a sales pitch, it became a venture into transformation.

And that is the other thing that I don't think people understand. When those drug dealers pulled up and got out of their jeep, strolled up to the house and realized that something had seriously changed. It changed the frequency of that block and that neighborhood. They looked at each other, they looked at their jeep, they looked at the house and they got back into their jeep and left because they knew that they were not welcome there. (George J. , How I got started, 2012)

John has the ability to see a different reality with his heart and soul. Some may call it a premonition, but others will say that he wills his vision into reality. The vision of a healthy neighborhood was just the beginning of that reality. If it were possible to have a personal relationship with a non-living entity or object, for John that would be the building at 17405 Lahser. He has had a dance partnership with this building ever since Felix looked over at the vacant, dilapidated building and suggested that it could become the headquarters for their organization.

John remembers, "It was 21,000 square feet of blight and it took 1.4 million dollars to restore it. I paid a dollar for it and I had to borrow that dollar. If you can convince yourself to believe the impossible, anything is possible. I guess if you really want something badly enough you can will it into existence. That is what creating something out of nothing is all about to me." And "will it into existence" John did not once. but twice!   (George J. , How I got started, 2012)

After the purchase of the building in August of 1995 the volunteers set to work cleaning out the structure wheelbarrow by wheelbarrow.   When they weren't shoveling up debris they were tearing out windows, walls and ceilings.   It would take hundreds of volunteers and months of literally sweat, blood and dirt underneath the fingernails before the site would even be close to ready for the next phase.

Before anything could take place however, it was necessary to get funding in place, in other words, to "sell the vision". The building consisted of "7000 square feet of red maple floors but they were all pretty much warped and had to be restored. The windows were broken, there was a hole in the roof, all of the electrical, plumbing, heating and cooling had been striped. It had been vacant for 15 to 20 years, it was just a wreck. Before it could be operational we had to touch every square inch from the roof to the gutters to the sewers to the pipes." (George J. J., How it all Got Started,

2012)   As one can imagine people do not come knocking on your door to give you a check. You must wine and dine your prospects or in John's case you have to paint a picture, tell a story or as John and Johnson put it you have to "fake it until you make it" or "props and picks".

After the initial loan from Bank One of $875,000 was almost gone, funding that provided for the very infrastructure of the building, the remainder of the funds came from a smorgasbord of sources, private, corporate and civic sectors. (Comerica Bank, Fanny Mae, Ford Motor Company, Sears, Kmart, GM, Chrysler and others) To invite folks to invest their money in something that might seem like a pipe dream, it would take some real acting. It was like a Laurel and Hardy slap stick, as John describes, "We were out of money and with only eleven thousand left, we had to think fast." A representative from Fanny Mae was coming over and John wanted to show this investor something significant to demonstrate how wisely the precious funds were being invested into a worthy project. Currently the center was just one big room, the space had been had insulated and dry-walled the ceiling and had been stripped and scrapped but that was it. Kevin Johnson, a man who had become John's best friend and right hand man on this journey recalls how the Laurel and Hardy act played out. "John looked at me and said "Mr. Johnson, you know what we are going to do, we are going to paint every wall in this room white and we are going to have the floor guy come in and redo all the floors."

"John I don't think that's the right decision, we still have all this work yet to do and the polished floors will be destroyed. John 's response was, 'I know what I am doing, follow my lead, don't think. Just do what I say, don't even think.' 'Ok John, ok.' When he got those floors finished it was the most beautiful thing. He just had that image in his head. 7000 square feet of hardwood floors. He said, 'Just wait until you see.' When I saw it , Wow! It looked like a basketball court, it was just one big room with white walls and a beautiful floor. I like to compare it to an artist whitewashing a canvas so that people can dream, some people can't dream through dust and broken windows they need more. So we had new windows put in, the walls painted, the ceiling dry-walled and the floors finished. It was incredible!"

Just as Kevin was washing the last brush in walked the representatives from Fanny Mae people walked through the door. They were stunned and impressed and before leaving that day they committed to contributing $100,000 to the remaining project. The Laurel and Hardy act was a success!

Some funds came in assigned to specific projects within the structure. The kitchen was just one of those such projects, Masco Corporation contributed a quarter million dollars just to restore the kitchen. Another $250,000 came from the cities Community Development Block Grant/Neighborhood Opportunity Fund (NOF) while other dollars came from Comerica, Ford Motor, Sears, Kmart, GM, Chrysler to name just a few of the many funders."

As funds came in the next phase of the building plan would be completed until eventually it was time to

John George is like a coach of a football team. He always has the whole picture in mind.

Orchestrating excellent plays. A leader, I admire that about him.

(Carter, 2012)

set up shop. The community center didn't just house the Blight Buster organization but other non-profit agencies that either collaborated with the Blight Buster program or were partners in the community vision of revitalizing the area.

The significance of this community center cannot be fully comprehended until you understand that when the "building opened in November of 2000, the 8th Precinct had closed their doors, the YMCA had gone to a private charter and the library had closed. The Motor City Resource Center, as it was known then, saved this community. This became a hub for services, outreach and community building.

"If you can convince yourself to believe the impossible, anything is possible."

5

Programs and Projects

If I had a hammer,
I'd hammer in the morning,
I'd hammer in the evening,
All over this land,
I'd hammer out danger,
I'd hammer out a warning,
I'd hammer out love between,
My brothers and my sisters,
All over this land.
Peter, Paul & Mary - If I Had A
Hammer
Lee Hayes and Seeger Pete

If the structure of a house is created from framing and a human body is composed of systems, then it could be considered that an organization is structured through its use of programs or projects. For a mission or vision to take shape and evolve it must move beyond one individual's conceptualization. The originator of the idea must be able to convey the message to others in such a way that they not only understand the mission but are so moved that they want to be included and take ownership of the concept as well. This takes a person with charisma, a person who can paint a picture so compelling and moving that others are hooked before they realize what has happened. That surely describes John. Anyone who has ever heard his "war cry" knows he has a way of drawing people in.

Once the mission is conveyed and the people are moved its time to give them something to do. Oftentimes, this is where a passion or a dream loses its momentum. If there are no actions, no tasks for people to become involved in, the organization never expands beyond the idea stage. This is where John's additional attributes come into play.

One of John's most significant traits is his extraordinary skill as an organizer. His mother, recalls that when he was just a young boy he would find cleaning the garage not a chore but a fun enterprise. John is a man who envisions things working better if there is a plan in place and an organized approach. Now there must be a caveat here: anyone who knows John also knows that many of his endeavors are initiated and navigated by faith and a little prayer, and accomplished through an act of God. So while he likes to run a 'tight ship" he often opts for in-the-moment inspiration and last-minute planning to pull off the impossible. Because, as John will tell you, "It is all about making the impossible, possible." With that said, however, it would be his preference to have a plan, assemble the team and orchestrate an operation. These three components form the framework for programs, and projects that help build an organization.

As John's vision took shape, projects were created and programs were launched and the organization, Motor City Blight Busters was born. But if programs and projects are the framework for an organization then its mission, goals, and strategic plan would be the blueprint for

> Blight Busters is a good solution to what is going on in the city. They are a just do it company, they don't just wait around and talk about how things are, they get out and bust some sweat and do it. They are always working hard and that is what we need in the cities and communities.
>
> **Dakarai Carter, Christ the Redeemer Summer Mission, 2012**

that structure. This new organization planned to take a

simple neighborhood cleanup effort and transform it into a full-blown "revitalization" operation. The Merriam Webster Dictionary defines revitalization as "to give new life or vigor to." The Blight Buster plan defines this new sense of "life" more concretely as: home restoration and sale, home construction and sale, building demolition, neighborhood clean –up/ beautification, and education and skills training. Throughout its 25-year history, Blight Busters has indeed covered all of those areas and then some.

The first program that Motor City Blight Busters launched has become its cornerstone: demolition, the face and the embodiment of Blight Busters. It was the volunteers' ability to embrace John's vision by actually taking the axes and

sledgehammers and tearing down eyesores that made them feel connected. They felt that they had literally flung themselves into this fight for justice, and at the end of the day they could feel that they had indeed made a

"I think this experience has been a great one. I have learned so much from so many people. Just like helping out the community. It always makes me feel good. I love doing anything I can to make Detroit and the surrounding areas a better place."

Sasha Tremblay, Christ the Redeemer Summer Mission 2012

difference.

So how does one take down a house? There is a process and a plan. To the volunteer it may appear that you just go up to the first firebombed house you see and with your ax in hand start "swingin". In reality, there are quite a few steps that take place before that ax is swung.

In the early days when John was still just cleaning the streets and helping his friends and neighbors, it would all begin with a phone call or a neighbor coming by and giving him a hand only to ask, "Can you do this with the house next door to me?" So sure enough, a few neighbors would gather and - board-by-board, shingle-by-shingle - the house would be dismantled and pulled down. Through the years, John learned what to do and what not to do, with trial and error being the best teacher. Each demolition helped to define the plan and process and today. Today, John's son, John William George, Blight Buster's Site Manager, oversees this part of the operation, from the first phone call to the last dumpster. According to John William a project begins when, "someone calls and says 'There is this old house, can you take it down?" or 'There's a garage in my neighbor's yard and I don't like the way it looks it's not safe'. Or someone will call and say, 'There've been people in and out of this house during the night and it scares us.' Or someone will just donate the house to us." (George,

2012)

The next step in the process is assessing how to proceed: does the house get rehabbed, or does it move on to demolition? A house is evaluated based on the soundness of the structure. If it is brick or cider block, there is usually a substantial foundation to restore. A wood frame house is more often compromised; and, given the original poor construction methods used on many of the homes in this area, it will most likely move on to the demolition track quickly.

John William George has spent his childhood and teen years refining demolition to an art. Watching John William - whether it be on the roof swinging the ax, or at the base of the house directing volunteers as crew leader and site manager - its obvious, that like his father he commands the respect and attention of the volunteers as he directs with confidence. His knowledge has been gained through years of practice and wisdom passed on through his father's counsel and direction.   As manager, John William oversees the entire process of preparing the site for demolition - from attaining all the permits and permissions to acquiring the necessary funding.   To initiate this process, the structure's ownership must be first identified. While this is simple when the property has been donated, it is much more complicated when it has been abandoned.

Abandoned properties materialize in a few different ways, the less common but more straightforward being through foreclosure, an estate without heirs, or forfeiture for overdue taxes. Most times however, it is a lot more complicated. Dennis Archer, former Mayor of the City of Detroit, describes the demise this way: "When people were leaving their houses and they couldn't sell them, they started renting. They wouldn't put money into their property, so each time a person left the property it was in less than best condition, and then they took less money for rent. Ultimately, when it became run down the owners walked away from it." (Archer, May)

In cases where the owners are impossible to locate, once all attempts of finding them have been exhausted, the City will turn over the abandoned property. Next, requests are made to turn off the gas, electricity and water, oftentimes incurring fees for unpaid utility bills. Showing proof of all these actions will lead to acquisition of the demolition permits.

At this point, it's hard to imagine why one "crazy" man would even continue this convoluted journey. Probably because his motto is: "When you believe in the impossible anything is possible." At this point John recounts "We'll go and look at the house. If it is in decent shape we will hire a rehab company to come in and rehab the house and sell it to a low-income family. If there is water or fire damage; a roof is missing, or there is nothing we can do to fix it without spending a million dollars, then we will just tear it down." (George, 2012)

The next step is actually part of the ongoing administrative arm of the organization - fund-raising. Funds for the project may come from the annual budget for revitalizations. If it is a project that hasn't been budgeted for then funds will have to be raised prior to beginning the demolition, or perhaps even earlier, to pay for permits, utilities and outstanding taxes.

"For us to legally take these down there are quite a few steps." John shares, "You have to acquire the property; you have to get the deed; you have to clear the taxes, the encumbrances, the light bill, the water bill, the gas bill. It's a complicated process. DTE will allow you to disconnect all of the electrical and not charge you. But their sister, Mich Con, charges $850 per address to disconnect the gas. So there are a lot of costs just to be in position to dismantle, demolish, deconstruct, recycle. It's a bit of a process." (George J. , 2012)

Once the funds and permits are in place, the next step in the journey is to prepare the site. Before volunteers arrive on the scene it's important to be sure that the "City actually came out and turned off the gas, electricity and water; then you can order your dumpsters" and call in the volunteers.

(George J. W., 2012)   The first task for the volunteers is clearing out the debris left behind.   There are those items that are natural features of a home - sinks, cupboards, carpeting, toilets, bathtub, and of course the monstrous heating system - that all need to be pulled.   While these fixtures are cumbersome and at times a challenge, it is the previous resident's personal effects that are probably the most time-consuming to remove.   These include clothing, furniture, televisions, books, toys, food, and tools or recreational equipment, which are strewn throughout the building.   If the house has been firebombed, as is usually the case, all of this is waterlogged, moldy and weighs a ton. With a little ingenuity and cleverness this tedious task becomes an adventure.   John and his team give general direction and safety guidelines, but allow the volunteers to decide on their own terms what they want to tackle and how they want to go about it.   This contributes to a very carnival like atmosphere, which is of little wonder since the whole concept of this vaudeville act grew from those early carnivals and wonderlands held in John's garage and backyard during his childhood.   If a passerby should stop, at first glance they would sense chaos - but upon a closer look they would laugh at the novelty of it all.   As one person takes a practical approach using a wheelbarrow to maneuver items back and forth from house to dumpster, others enthusiastically stuff assorted toys and collectibles into pillowcases, while another will grab an old pot and carry out exploding cans of swollen and charred food. Meanwhile, the jokester is in his glory, carrying out a lampshade on his head with a curtain rod in his hand as he proclaims this his Kingdom and marches through the crowd.

Yes, it is a spectacle to behold but amazingly, when the day is done, the house has been cleared. With John's direction, the carpeting has been pulled and the floors swept and all the remnants of a life once lived have been cleared and are compressed into two, three, four or more dumpsters. John fastidiously keeps the site clear of loose debris and the site sets ready and waiting for the next step. This first step is more grueling when the house is filled with a lifetime of "junk". Many times these abandoned homes are stuffed from floor to ceiling with books, newspapers, mail, and the assorted trappings of a hoarder. These sites may take many attempts to prepare for demolition with several groups of volunteers, not to mention additional dumpsters (which are costly at five hundred dollars a hit). It is important to note that no two worksites are the same. While the work is most times predictable, there is always an element of surprise along the way.

Demolition is like a three-act play: gutting and dismantling, pulling down the structure, and disassembling the roof and flooring. This performance is accompanied by a symphony of sound - hammers and axes crescendo with voices and shouts. Wood cracking, pipes clanging and the blasts of car horns proclaiming their praises add the percussion to this scene.

The first act opens with windows and doors being knocked out and carried to the dumpster. The scene changes quickly and the audience sees a swarm of cast members descending upon the outer shell. The actors ferociously tear at the siding with their bare hands as if on a mission to discover a treasure - ripping at the aluminum covering, pealing it off in layers and discarding it at their feet. Right behind them is the second wave of actors ready to snatch up the panels and cart them away. The stage is humming and it seems that the cast is growing in size. There is a buzzing of activity taking place within the structure and within seconds debris is being hoisted through the openings where the windows once hung. Two-by-fours and wall sections are being carried out the front door to the dumpster, while the porch that the workers are stepping across is being dismantled by another lively crew. As the exterior covering is finally removed, the audience is awed to

At the end of the day after all the dirt, debris and the sledge hammers John let me help hook a chain to one of the beams in the house, and then to his truck. Watching that house crash to the ground gave me such a sense of accomplishment. Not only from all the hard work, but for the contribution to the future of Detroit.

Mandy Sabo

see the heightened activity taking place within: the interior walls have been removed and the last of the interior framework is being knocked out.

Then the curtain is pulled, everything stops outside, the participants step back as the second scene opens.   The Blight Buster crew takes over and they begin weakening the remaining structure, removing every other two-by-four. Breathless the audience wonders if the structure will collapse right before their eyes. Then things get serious very quickly. The Blight Busters crew are in the spotlight now and they take their directions strictly from the star, the one that everyone has been waiting to catch a glimpse of. Directed to weaken one exterior wall a couple crew move in while another maneuver a heavy crude chain into place. With some consultation the chain is wrapped around a corner support with the other end carefully fastened to the frame of a heavy-duty pickup truck.

Onlookers are in awe as the star of this production gives the engine of the two-ton truck full throttle. The truck trembles like a teakettle about to give off steam, the house creaks and then there is the unmistakable snap as the first two-by-four pops. The site is alive with commotion, for those first-time attendees it is but a blur. In one sweeping motion the ground shakes and the structure crashes in on itself.   The audience is spellbound, transfixed by the image of splintering wood and the plume of dust that is now cascading down upon them. Someone coughs and the spell is broken. Their faces reflect disbelief as they realize that the house is down. It is as if they missed the whole scene. They are in shock, but only for a moment because this climax throws the audience right into the final scene of this three-act production. The seasoned veterans are already on the heap of rubble, cloaked in the dust that is still making its way to the ground. With axes in full swing they eagerly chop away at the mass of wood and shingles.

An organization's programs and projects emerge either as an element of the original plan, as a goal that is developed, or through a specific need that arises. "Clean Sweep" is a project that grew out of the original plan to keep the streets clean, and in time it took shape as an annual campaign. What John had begun as a simple effort to just sweep the streets of Northwest Detroit for those first six years, took on a citywide scope as the City awakened to the idea of revitalization. "I was impressed with what John was doing. He and his *'crew'* - I use this as a term of endearment - would go out and they would pick an area, or a house, or a couple of houses that were incapable of being repaired, and they would tear them down. In some instances they would even rehabilitate where that was possible, to try to put people into the homes." (Archer, May)

It was this that inspired Mayor Dennis Archer, to challenge

the people of the city to take their neighborhoods back - starting with their own front yards. "When I made my remarks in the inauguration, I asked people to clean up in front of their homes and take the debris out of the streets so that it wouldn't clog up the drains. Out of that we came up with the idea to pick a weekend and clean up the city and parks and we called it Operation Clean Sweep. We had businesses that would help us by giving us brooms, rakes, garbage bags, and gloves. I remember it was so infectious that Dave Breck, who was Oakland County Circuit Court Judge, came and worked. Oakland County Executive L. Brooks Patterson sent some equipment in to be of help. Of course, we had our own folks in terms of the DPW. We cleaned up and fixed up." Detroit Clean Sweep, as it is now referred to, is an annual event held in early May each year. (Archer, May)

Keeping the streets clean is important - but keeping the streets safe is essential, and was ultimately behind everything John was doing. It is no secret that since the 1980s, Detroit had been fighting a sometimes losing battle with arson and crime on the three days preceding Halloween. The old idea of horseplay and tricks from an earlier time-when children TP and egged houses, and wrote on windows with wax, had been replaced with lighting abandoned houses ablaze, shootings, robberies and other assorted criminal acts. The term "Devil's Night" was taking on a very literal interpretation. In 1984, at the height of the mêlée, there were 800 fires reported during that three-day period. Then Mayor, Coleman Young, organized "his appointees, volunteers and neighborhood community groups across the city to come out for three nights and volunteer to make sure the city no longer had the fires." (Archer, May)

While the City continued to soldier its response to the crime and arson with its own plan of action, John was busy recruiting forces from the playing field. If this was a chess game, John would be winning the play. His strategy was to arm the people who had a stake in reclaiming their homes and neighborhoods with the tools they needed to protect their homes, property and families - flashlights, vests and walkie-talkies. What began with a handful of neighbors has now grown into a citywide initiative with thousands of people coming out to take back the streets. John began organizing community patrols to protect the neighborhoods from Devil's Night crime in 1989 about the same time that he acquired an International Harvester ambulance that looked like something out of the '60s and was very similar to the vehicle popularized by the movie *Ghost Busters*. Putting two and two together, the vehicle was christened the "Blight Buster".

Originally, this crusade to protect the streets was an extension of a neighborhood watch and patrol. It wasn't until John's Aunt Mary shared her feelings about the term "Devil's Night" that the "Devil" was taken out of the Halloween picture and God and his angels were put in charge and out front.

> *I was at my Aunt Mary's house and it was just a couple days before "that other name" night and she was all upset, and, I said 'Aunt Mary what is wrong?' And she said; 'That darn Devil's night is coming and I hate it. I wish they would get rid of it.' That was when a light went off in my head. 'Let's call it Angels' Night'. She said, 'that would be great', and I said; 'I tell you what, from here on out, we won't use that other name we will call it Angels' Night.' So I went back to the office and I wrote a press release, called the media and did a number of things to launch the Angels' Night campaign. It took us a couple years, but we used the media to leverage the concept and ultimately got Mayor Archer to take it citywide. Channels 2, 4, and 7 were using the terms interchangeably initially and by the end of the 1996 Halloween holiday they unanimously chose "Angels' Night." It was official!* (George J. J., 2011)

From that point on, the nights before Halloween became Angels' Nights and the patrols have successfully transformed this time of evildoing into a community banded together, working and celebrating to bring peace and safety to their community. The City of Detroit embraced John's insightful terminology of "Angels' Night" and, under the mayoral leadership of Dennis Archer, took this positive campaign citywide in 1995.

In January 2011, a program and partnership was launched to help new parolees gain a foothold back into society. Working with AmeriCorps and the Michigan Prisoner Reentry Program, Blight Busters provided the group a home base and transportation - not to mention full immersion into the revitalization efforts taking place in the northwest corner of Detroit. Through the nine-month duration of the program 20 men participated - offering them an opportunity to not only earn some income but also to gain valuable volunteer experience. "Two days a week they worked in the community, and three days they were here helping renovate homes to move in low income families," Steve Anderson, then Program Manager for Blight Busters, shares.

As the AmeriCorps worker for the project, Steve coordinated all the day-to-day activities of the program. "I would go with them to the homes and help them paint, while teaching them something about carpentry. We would also take them to the DIA along with community colleges to fill out applications. Out of 20, 16 of them ended up going back to college!" (Anderson, 2012) "The mission of the Michigan Prisoner Reentry Program is to significantly reduce crime and enhance public safety by implementing a seamless system of services for offenders - from the time of their entry to prison through their transition, community reintegration and aftercare in their communities." (Michigan.gov) "While short lived this site had an 80 percent". recidivism rate." (Anderson, 2012) Due to cuts in state and federal funding the program ended in October, 2011 - but not before having an immeasurable impact on 20 young men who were afforded a second chance with a group of people who were committed to helping them succeed on this new direction in their lives.

Anderson recalls how, for one young man, the difference impacted every aspect of his life. "This 22-year-old father of two young children had been out of prison four months after serving a five-year term. He came in and was loud and boisterous, and didn't really want to take part in what the program was offering. After he saw that Blight Busters and the AmeriCorps team had a vested interest in what they were doing, he began to come around. He was always the first one there for volunteer events and he took every opportunity to do extra Saturday events. They were required to do 200 hours of community service and then they were done. But he went above and beyond that to do about 250 hours. The last time I spoke to him he was taking two classes per semester and working at the same time."

The program also provided participants the opportunity to

acquire a food handlers license so they could work in the food service business. This allowed the young man to get a fulltime job working at a restaurant in Detroit. Through the AmeriCorps program he earned his GED, and then went on to attend classes at Henry Ford Community College. "So he had a fulltime job, was taking two classes and had returned to his two children, being fully impactful in a positive way in their lives."

When programs are created that have such an all-encompassing impact on people's demonstrates just how powerful an organization and a vision can be.

Most Blight Buster projects grow out of a need: an eyesore needs to be eliminated, a homeowner needs help saving her house, a vacant lot or park is overgrown and unsafe. However, every once in awhile, someone comes to John with an idea, an inspiration and a wish to share these resources with the community to help create more positive energy. Such was the case with David Bess, an American sculptor known for his eccentric design and altruistic approach to art and life. Bess's use of recycled materials to build precarious structures he calls "temples" (Temple of Joy, Temple of the Mind), gained notoriety in 2001 when he created the *Temple of Tears*, a memorial for a friend who was killed in a motorcycle accident. The sculpture evolved into a place of ritual in where friends would leave prayers, memorabilia, pictures and even ashes of their loved ones.

The structure was no longer something to just look at but a symbol of life that would draw thousands of pilgrims. The pilgrims would gather at this shrine each year for an event which became appropriately known as, the Burning Man Festival. The shrine, an assemblage of papier-mâché and metal would be set ablaze ceremoniously as the group gathered round and watched as the mass of sticks, paper and random matter, grew into an enormous bonfire, a burning prayer with a spirit of its own to those looking on.

Bess's work became a collaborative enterprise with the Black Rock Arts Foundation, (BRAF) a group focused on cultivating public artwork to build and empower community. It was only a matter of time and providence until this collective group would find its way to Northwest Detroit. In the summer of 2008, Bess's travels brought him to Detroit and it was just a few short connections before he was introduced to John and his vision of saving this small community.

It all started with a meeting of the minds: Bess and his team coordinated with the local BRAF Chapter, a crew of Detroit burners (those who build artistic structures to burn), and everyone got to talking. "I told them, if you think we are so heroic," Bess proclaims to his team who reside out on the western side of the country, "take a look around here. There's no threat in the desert anymore—I'm in an air-conditioned Airstream, eating caviar and drinking champagne. Let's build something here where there are real challenges. Let's grab some land and build something."

Where to build was a question that didn't take long to answer. It was a site that had previously been an abandoned house turned crack house - a building that was situated adjacent to Motor City Blight Busters headquarters. The house had been a retail space for a pseudo mattress outlet, while hosting nefarious individuals, becoming its own source of decay. "Things were taking place on those mattresses that would horrify you," John recalls. "Drinking, smoking, drugs, prostitution, all types of things."

One night the negative energy erupted into a massive blaze that engulfed the structure reducing it to ash. The Blight Busters team quickly cleared the land and created a small community park. A year later teens from Christ the Redeemer Catholic Church in Lake Orion planted a Peace Pole on the spot. It was ceremoniously unveiled while launching the Angels' Night patrol in 2005. The pole was inscribed with the word "peace" in four languages: English, Spanish, Braille and Swahili. Prayer and a community spirit blessed this park as a sacred place where the people of the neighborhood could gather for picnics, barbeques and fellowship.

When Bess saw this spot and heard its story, he knew this

was where the temple would be built. Mark Higbie, a BRAF member and former Detroiter, understood the relevance of building the Bess Temple at this specific location. "Peace Park sits at the nexus of both the hope and sorrow of Detroit," He explains.

Over the next several months, Bess, BRAF and John met to coordinate details and supplies. Each of Bess's structures are composed of recycled materials from the local area. This structure, however, would hold more than local materials. Bess found an intricate pattern located in California that he thought would best fit the image he had envisioned for Peace Park. This structure would not be burned, in this community where fires had been the symbol of decay, this structure would be built to remain as a sacred place for all the community to come to and celebrate life. This would not be a Burning Man, but a true Temple of Peace.

Although it may have taken a couple of months to coordinate and pull the supplies together, the temple took only one week to build. It was like an old town barn raising - everyone from near and far gathered to create a community temple, a place that was home to all, a sacred symbol of peace.

John recalls the event, a festival in its own rite: "Fifty of us came together and a tent city was built where we would all live and sleep for the duration of the project. There was a barbeque pit, a DJ and a cooler full of whatever. We started on Saturday and ended the following Saturday, working 12-hour days. Different folks would come and go, it would ebb and flow as it took shape."

Many of the people who helped with the project lived in the surrounding neighborhoods, while some came from across the country, even as far as Hawaii. The group was eclectic, filled with folks of every personality and from every walk of life. Some were artists, some were advocates of justice and some were professional tradesmen, but all were builders of hope, a theme that united them and emanated an energy that gave this temple its heart and sealed within it the message of peace.

The BRAF crew inspired the workers and shared the story behind the Bess temples. The idea that prayers and memorabilia would be entwined in the structure touched the volunteers, and as the work-week went on they each began to weave into their workspace memories of loved ones who had been lost to violence on the city streets. Erik Davis, board member of the Black Art Rocks Foundation writes in the article the Detroit Dream Project how David Bess recalls meeting Mr. Washington, the owner of the beauty parlor, located right across the street from the temple. When asked what was going on, Bess explained. "It's for celebrations, weddings, memorials. Say a kid graduates from high school with honors, they can come here to recognize him. It's a place for the community to meet and congregate."

"Washington then told Bess that his brother had just died in prison, and that his friends and family were planning to hold a memorial in a nearby church. Bess offered to inscribe the brother's name on a piece of wood, and give Washington a ride up in the forklift so he could nail the plank up top. That way he could see his brother's name from his shop. But Washington didn't want to go up. 'Do you know the gospel song, A Closer Walk With Thee?' Bess asked. 'Sure I do.' Washington responded. 'Well if you go up in the lift you will be closer to the Lord and closer to your brother.' Mr. Washington laughed. 'You're gonna make me go up there, aren't you?' And when he came down off the lift, Bess offered him the use of the temple for the memorial service. 'Your brother died in a building. You don't need to bring his spirit back into another building. Come here and do it outside.' (Davis)

And so, one by one, the volunteers nailed their messages of sorrow and hope within the structure. John recalls a couple who worked there throughout the week, "They came every day and worked and were our best volunteers ever. I couldn't understand why they were working so hard, but I found out that Saturday, when we finished about noon.

The woman had seen this project as a way to pay tribute to her son who had been killed. During the week, the man who had stood by her side had proposed to her, and it was decided what better way to pay tribute and honor him than to be married right there at the sight that gave hope. "So, at 3 o'clock on the final day of the event, they got married under the temple christening the Peace Temple with positive energy that has flowed ever since."

Since that beautiful day, the park and temple have stood as a nexus of hope and positive energy. It is here each October that Angels' Night launches its now famous night patrols, and a space where poetry readings and gospel fests are held. On a warm summer's night, this is where the smell of charcoal wafts through the air as burgers sizzle on barbeque grills, layered with the sounds of a jazz ensemble calling all together to laugh, tell stories and be family.

"I guess if you really want something badly enough you can will it into existence.

That is what creating something out of nothing is all about to me."

COMPASSIONATE 6

And the King will reply,

"Truly I tell you, whatever you did for one of the least of these brothers and sisters of mine, you did it for me."

MATTHEW 25:40

This story, about a man named John Joseph George, is not just about a person or his accomplishments, but an attempt to identify what it is that fuels a passion, a life commitment such as this. It's about that burn, deep within that grows and grows until it takes control of a person's being. It is about what drives a person to sacrifice, not just the creature comforts we all enjoy - a nice dinner, nice clothes, freedom to take time to relax, visit friends and take vacations; but a passion that creates sacrifice so intense that even personal human needs such as, food, warm clothing, a roof overhead, and precious time with family are shunned in order to fulfill the vision. What fills a man with such selflessness as this?

A cold, drizzling, damp day greeted John as he arrived at the project site wearing just a business suit coat over his customary Blight Busters t-shirt. A volunteer asked, "Hey, John, do you have a meeting to go to?" Grabbing a sledgehammer he shook his head saying "No." The volunteer, not satisfied, asked, "But you're wearing a suit coat. What's with that?" He responded matter-of-factly as he continued working, "I gave my coat away last week to someone who needed it more than me."

Yes, that is John, never thinking of himself. His daughter Ann Marie said, "I buy him coats, boots, clothes all the time. The following week, I come by and they are gone.

He has given them away to someone else who needed them more than him, he says." That is just who John is. It doesn't matter if he needs it or not, he thinks only of the other person. "He has respect for every single person he encounters. " (George A. M., 2011)

John the Compassionate. There is no shortage of stories when we look at John's kindness to others.

He never thinks about himself, he is constantly doing whatever he can to make his hometown a great place to live in. He never takes time for himself, it is always about others.

Sara Tremblay, Summer Mission Volunteer from Christ the Redeemer Church, Lake Orion, Michigan.

It is seen in the simple act of offering someone a ride or listening to someone's story with an empathetic ear. John reaches out every day to the people on the streets of Detroit. No one is a stranger to John's outreached hand.

John's good friend Todd McKler remembers when he was down on his luck and out of money. He had an infant son and his refrigerator had just quit working. "I called John and he said, 'Hang on, Todd. I'll make a few calls.' He made a few calls and got with a couple of guys, and they came to my rescue. John said, 'Okay, we found you a fridge. You just need to go to St. Vincent de Paul and pick it up.' And I said, 'I appreciate you finding it and like I explained before, I don't have the money to pay you back.' It wasn't long and they were at my house. We all went to the St. Vincent de Paul down there off of Gratiot and we picked up this fridge. They didn't want me even to help lift it. I asked, 'Why are you doing this for me?' Then they got to my house and unloaded it, got it set up, and they shook my hand and said, 'Have a nice day.' These guys are like angels. Who do you know who would do something like that at the last minute?" (McKler, 2012)

That is the way John works. His deep compassion is as much a part of him as his name. Sometimes John's certitude to do the right thing can go as far as saving another man's dignity. Kevin Johnson, now John's right hand man and best friend, was a stranger when John came upon him working at one of those quick oil change businesses. John had brought his car in for servicing and struck up a conversation with Kevin. It turned out they had a mutual friendship with Felix. About two weeks later, they met again - this time at Farmer Jack where Kevin had just been hired - a step up from his job at the oil change center. John quickly assessed the situation and said, "I just saw you at the oil change shop and now you're working here. You seem like a guy who doesn't mind working. I want you to work for me." And that is how their partnership and friendship began. Kevin continued his job at Farmer Jack while working weekends with John.

Some time later, when Kevin had moved on to a construction job and was continuing to juggle his weekends working with John misfortune crossed his path. Kevin had lost his license, and after being picked up for driving on a suspended license, was faced with a $1,000 fine or 90 days in jail. He explained to the judge that he would need to continue working in order to pay the fine. With John and his wife advocating for him, a work release arrangement was reached, allowing him to work during the day and serve his time in the evenings. Things didn't go as planned, though. When Kevin returned to his job with Farmer Jack, after having missed 10 days due to his time in jail, he was informed he no longer had a job. The parole officer did not accept this news favorably, and demanded that Kevin return to the jail immediately.

Kevin was beside himself, not knowing where to turn for help or what to do next. So he did the only thing he could think of and called John. John took a look at Kevin's paperwork and filled it out, indicating that he was working full time at Blight Busters. Kevin worked the rest of the day and returned that night with the paperwork complete and a full-time job. Kevin's life was forever changed, and to this day he is dedicated to John and his mission. Reflecting, Kevin softly sighs, "I just love that guy."

The list of people whom John has impacted is endless, and

could be a book in itself. John has changed lives and destinies for many, many people. One such person was Mama Gloria, who is herself an enigma. This women with a smile that lights the world and a heart of equal measure was born just outside of New York City, but grew up in the woods of northern Michigan in a little town called Idlewild. This little hamlet was a resort for the African American elite including, artists, entertainers and athletes. During the late forties and fifties Gloria spent her summers helping her family earn a living by selling firewood to the tourists who were there for vacation. Influenced by the great artists, Gloria went on to create her own art - first as a hair stylist in New York for affluent African American women, then writing plays, performing spoken word and creating stained glass windows. She was a most gifted women to be sure.

In her later years, Gloria retired to her much beloved Lillicrest homestead in Idlewild. While the notoriety of Idlewild lived in the hearts of many, the big theatres and dance halls it had once been famous for were long gone. Here where jazz and blues once wafted through the air, Mama Gloria's home sat nestled in the woods, a respite for artists of today. She had a studio for her glass and fine arts and a stage for performing, but it was her warmth and kind spirit that welcomed frequent visitors.

But fate would take its toll on Mama Gloria. One evening as she was sleeping, a fire brewed in her home. By the time she awoke, it was all she could do to save herself. Her home was destroyed, along with all her art and belongings. Gathering up what few possessions she could recover, she took up residence in the home she grew up in, which remained on the property. The loss was too much though and she soon became fraught with sickness. Her livelihood stood in a heap of burnt remains in front of her, a constant reminder of what her life had once been.

It was during this time that John and a crew of very energetic teens came out to help. Mama Gloria was no stranger to John or Chaz Miller, an artist and organic gardener, she had volunteered at the Village sharing her own passion of art through the years. So when John and the Blight Busters team heard of her sad situation, they gathered the troops and were off to help.

The teens from Christ the Redeemer Catholic Church in Lake Orion, Michigan, had been working with John during the summers for some years and when they heard Mama Gloria's story they made a commitment to join John on this new mission and venture. Spending an entire weekend cleaning the site, the group gave Mama Gloria new hope. By the end of the weekend the grounds were restored, and everyone was enjoying their time together being inspired by one another. Mama Gloria literally glowed with hope for her little hostel as it lit up with the energy of the young people.

While John has been known to perform miracles with his crew, there is only so much anyone can do when it comes to health.   Mama Gloria was in the late stages of stomach cancer and her time at Lilliecrest and on this earth were coming to a close.   Despite her failing health John gave Mama Gloria a sense of hope and purpose. When Mama Gloria left her earthly vessel, she knew that Lilliecrest was alive and well and her dream of an artists' colony would not die with her.

Stories of John's compassion abound, hearing these stories told and retold creates a strong sense that John's gift for reaching out to others is beyond his own doing, that heavenly intervention is somehow at work, his son, John William recalls just such a time.   It was a collaborative effort among the community leaders on a mission to find the perfect family for a home that the Blight Busters crew had just renovated.   This home that sits on Grandview Street had been outfitted with "a new hot water tank and furnace; the hardwood floors had been redone; a new washer, dryer, refrigerator and stove had been installed, along with mini blinds on the windows and landscaping around the house, with the addition of a beautiful porch." The committee members - a local rabbi, priest and minister, along with John George diligently reviewed the one thousand applications they had received for consideration as recipients of this beautifully renovated home. Just prior to the formation of the selection process, a woman facing trials and tribulations of her own had happened upon John's front doorstep. An'aLese, a single mother of four, was living in her car, in desperate need of a place she could call home to provide her family with the stability they needed to grow and thrive. John encouraged her to submit her application to this campaign to find a homeowner for the newly renovated property.

John's compassion really knows no bounds. Anyone that knows John can tell a story of how he touched their life or that of someone they know. But John's love for life and respect for humanity does not end there it extends to all living things. Kevin tells this story: "We were going somewhere, and there was a dead dog on the road. John says, 'Well, Scruffy, I don't have time right now but I'll be back.' So we went back and took care of the animal. We found a plastic bag and I held the bag while John picked the animal up saying, 'We've got you, Scruffy; we've got you.' He didn't want to see him smashed. So he bagged him and buried him. He just isn't going to go past a dead dog. He'll say, 'Come on, Kevin, we have to go pick up a dog.'"

"John does not have a disingenuous bone in his body,"

Diana Jacokes

7

PARTNERSHIPS AND VOLUNTEERS

We're off to see the Wizard
The Wonderful Wizard of Oz
We hear he is a Whiz of a Wiz
If ever a Wiz there was
If ever, oh ever, a Wiz there was
The Wizard of Oz is one because
Because, because, because,
because, because
Because of the wonderful things
he does
We're off to see the wizard
The Wonderful Wizard of Oz!

A partnership is a relationship formed with the people behind an organization or business entity. Unlike the customary business relationship, a partnership is established through a more personal connection. It is a communion of like minds for the purpose of a common goal. Both parties have an ownership and a stake in the relationship and as a result, they both ultimately achieve a greater benefit than if they had set out on this endeavor as individual entities. The Motor City Blight Buster mission to "Save the world, starting with Detroit" and, more specifically, starting at the corner of Lahser and Grand River, would take many partnerships.

The partnerships that formed were not usually sought after; rather they evolved through personal relationships that John created as he did what he did each and every day. Whether it was the Elder walking down the street carrying his message of faith and salvation or the man behind the counter at the hardware store, each day John made new friendships that would be nurtured in time into partnerships.

Former Mayor, Dennis Archer puts it this way: "John recognized something he could make a difference in, and everybody just followed his pitch and believed in it." It is as if by osmosis the partners capture John's passion and are drawn into a sacred circle with the others. They believe so deeply in what they see, that they take on a shared ownership in the mission. They not only provide the resources they have agreed upon, but come back with their own hands and hearts to make a personal contribution. Part of this grows out of John's genuine way of welcoming everyone's ideas, talents and creative energy. No idea is dismissed. Instead, John encourages each and every person he meets to run with his or her idea and take it to wherever it may go.

Over the years, there's been a plethora of partnerships – partners whose contributions have been so significant that without them the face of Blight Busters would be an altogether different design and dimension. This account will focus on the partnerships that were key to three major initiatives on which John spent the greater part of his time and energy: the mission of revitalization, community outreach, and the Village. This is not intended to minimize the many others whose contributions are also critical to the mission of the Motor City Blight Busters; but it is necessary to keep the story focused and directed.

The Revitalization Mission

As John pulled his wagon down the street bearing his arsenal to fight the war on blight - a shovel, a rake and an axe - it wasn't long before the initial partnership was created. Felix Wright and Albert Mack were first on the scene, and as co-founders of the *Old Redford Clean-Up Association* set the stage for what was to become a decade-long mission to restore the Northwest corner of Detroit into a thriving and flourishing community again.

Before these three knew what they were getting themselves involved in, the next group of key players entered the picture. As the first crew of volunteers, elders from the Church of Jesus Christ of Latter-day Saints, formed a partnership that was pivotal in launching John's revitalization .

It was shortly after meeting the Elders that Jim Cope, along with the staff and employees of Alexander Hamilton Life Insurance, stepped onto the scene providing tools and funds that leveraged the first major cleanup event. This "crazy" project was just the sort of thing that the H.E.L.P., (Hamilton Employees Love People) group liked to get involved with. The group was instrumental in supplying the professional services needed to help John's organization attain the 501(c) (3) status to become an official nonprofit business.

Community Outreach

In 1999 Masco Corporation provided the necessary funds to contribute to the completion of the first two floors of the Motor City Blight Busters headquarters specifically focused on the construction of a fully operational commercial kitchen. After hearing about the work John was doing in Northwest Detroit, Masco sent over two of their associates to see just what John was doing. After giving them a tour of worksites and the Village, John took them through the main building that was serving as a Community Resource Center, ending up in the area that was to become the kitchen. He recalls, "It was just a big hole. I said, 'We want to have a community kitchen here with a dishwasher, a broiler and a freezer.' At the end of the tour they asked, 'How much will it cost?' I didn't know but I guessed, 'A quarter million dollars.' About two days later we had a check for $250,000, so be careful what you ask for!"

The kitchen provided opportunities to host large events both for fundraising purposes and celebrations, and was also outfitted to operate as a separate source of revenue for the organization.

John not only understands the importance of collaboration and partnerships, but he totally embraces them. In today's world where resources - physical, material and financial are in limited supply, it is critical to work with other organizations, businesses, institutions and governmental agencies to create any sort of substantial momentum toward change. It is impossible to use resources wisely without partnering. This is especially practical and essential on a governmental level.

Such was the case in 1992 when John met Dennis Archer. It was the year after Archer had announced that he was leaving his position on the Michigan Supreme Court and returning to practicing law. With the City's rising crime and financial woes, Archer felt it was time that he stepped in to take an active role in addressing the intensifying "problems being faced by the City." While Archer initiated a partnership with University of Michigan professors (a team he referred to as his "laboring oars") to research and create a proposal on how to turn the City around, John was in the streets pushing brooms and creating a movement from the grassroots. It was natural that their paths would cross.

When Archer sent out his proposal - a 56-page document entitled, *Thoughts for a Brighter Detroit*, to nonprofits and governmental agencies around the City, it was followed by a barrage a of townhall meetings. At one of these meetings John George met Dennis Archer. The idiom "great minds think alike" is a sentiment easily applied to these two passionate individuals who quickly began working together to make things happen throughout the City.

One of the most notable and powerful outcomes of their partnership was the evolution of the city-wide initiative program to address the three-day fire spree during the Halloween holiday. Mayor Archer shares, "My first year in office. I reported that the fires had spiked. At the end of three days, I said, 'I take the blame for that because we didn't have as many volunteers as Mayor Young had, but it will never happen again.' We had a huge force out the next year and by my last year in office we may have had 30,000 signed on as volunteers. Each year we kept reducing the fires until they were even lower than a normal day's fires." On the Northwest side of Detroit, John was carrying on his own campaign against the arsonists and decided to use angels against this devil's mayhem, launching the Angels' Night crusade.

"As I recall," Archer reflects, "it was John George who kept talking about Angel's Night and I agreed. It wasn't my idea. I think it was John George, quite frankly, who suggested changing the name. 'Mr. Mayor you ought to name this Angels' Night!' And so the City saw an incredible surge of positive energy and what had been a time of terror was turned into a City-wide neighborhood-to-neighborhood festival of hope and solidarity.

"We would have big rallies the Saturday before that three-day period. We would have schools, fire trucks and marching bands out there. We would go door-to-door to get people all signed up. After the second or third success we named it Angels' Night. We put the yellow lights on top of our cars. I did it! My wife did it. My sister-in-law, my friends, they were all out!" Archer shares with a smile and sense of pride. "The neighborhood precincts would host barbeques and potluck meals for the volunteers. "It was almost like an unwritten competition as to who would have the best food," Archer continues. Yes, indeed, these two like minds were transforming a City.

John's relationship with Archer took on an even more personal dimension when in the fall of 1997 Mayor Archer officiated the wedding ceremony of John and Monica White, John's second wife. As Mayor of the City of Detroit one of Archer's powers was that of officiating at marriage ceremonies. I would do this only "for people I really liked and admired," he confesses with a smile.

The Village

That symbiotic relationship is especially apparent as it is with those he's closest to, his business partners, Alicia Marion and Chazz Miller. Alicia's down to earth good nature demeanor attracted John at once and it wasn't long before the two had developed a friendship that would grow into a long-term intimate relationship and eventually marriage. Alicia understood John's passion, drive and unstoppable determination like no other women in his life. Alicia believed in what John was doing and became a compass for him. "Alicia is John's translator." Katrina Storm shares in the D Town Video. (Storm)"She takes this chaos and makes it breathable for us." Alicia was the stabilizing force John needed to move forward.

Just a few short months after they met Alicia was directing the Blight Busters operation from the inside, arranging for volunteers and maintaining the day-to-day details of the organization. Her keen business sense and her positive outlook were catalysts for John and the Motor City Blight Busters' mission to transform the corner of Lahser and Grand River. But there was a very significant and equally powerful vision at play here too - Alicia's dream, a dream to one day own her own coffee house. John's love for Alicia is immeasurable, and if he had a mind set to "save Detroit" it wasn't going to happen before he built the coffee shop of Alicia's dreams. The synergy of these two people fuels a momentum that is unstoppable.

Chazz Miller, with paint brush in hand, joined this dynamic duo in 2003, his vision of creating a space where artists could eat, gather, share and develop their talents sparked a fire within John George. The moment these two met it seemed they were destined to take the stabilization/revitalization mission to a whole new level. From the murals to the stage, this corner of the City was being transformed in ways unimaginable and John's humble vision to bring a sense of security and safety to the community took on a new direction and focus. Through Chazz's inspiration the Artist Village grew and blossomed into what has become a mecca for artists.

There are so many individuals that have contributed to the renewal of the City that its hard to know where to begin and end this exhaustive list. But one cannot stroll within or around the Village without catching sight of Kofi Royal, the Village's resident gardener. Kofe's vision for the sustainable community garden grew out of a response to an increasing problem. As Kofe describes it, the green spaces that were created after the removal of the blight now became "very attractive for dumping." (Royal, 2012) Building the community gardens in those spaces removed the prospect for additional blight while providing healthy, fresh vegetables and herbs to the people who lived nearby. The gardens also became a way to reconnect the residents with the land, teaching them how to grow their own fresh food.

It would be natural here to make mention of the newest partnership to come along, one with Michigan State University. Through the fall of 2010, while John explored his options to regain ownership of the main headquarters building, he also was meeting with Maria A. Ruemenabt at MSU, investigating the possibility of establishing an MSU extension office in this section of Detroit. Putting two and two together, John was quick to see how this could become a bargaining chip creating a viable plan for the old headquarters building.

As the powers to be came together, the building was purchased through the creation of a new entity, the Old Redford Development Corporation. Tom O'Brien, owner of the Brightmoor business, One Construction, Inc., has been a longtime neighbor and friend of Johns and an advocate of stabilizing the Northwest area of Detroit. John shares, "Thanks to Tom O'Brien, his wisdom and dollars, this building will be able to accept our tenant, Michigan State University. MSU wants to help us extend our garden into a farm The university known for its horticultural abilities plan to focus on nutritional food choices. In addition they want to create a 4-H club for the kids in the community." With the formation of this unique partnership, Michigan State University has become a stakeholder - not only in the long-term vision of creating urban farming - but more importantly, in establishing a resource center as a hub for the revitalization of this neighborhood and community.

Launching this program to operate alongside and in conjunction with the Blight Busters programs, Michigan State University is just one of the local universities that have signed on to support the mission and vision of the organization. Through the years, Eastern Michigan University, Wayne State University, the University of Michigan, and Oakland University have all provided volunteers and funding to help sustain the numerous Blight Busters programs and projects.

Partnerships can evolve from a brief encounter, or sometimes through a vision shared from one volunteer to another. Such was the case in early October 2011, when John was introduced to the Vice President of Operations for the Starbucks Corporation. The company was vetting Detroit for its National Conference, which would be attended by 10,000 people. Starbucks' mission to give back to the community is a commitment that is woven through the organization at all levels, from projects organized by individual cafes all the way up through the corporate headquarters. Naturally, it was part of the plan for the National Conference to include a service project for all of the 10,000 participants, a huge undertaking to say the least.

Seeking a non-profit organization that could find work for that many people, it wasn't long before Marty Cook, Regional Director of Operations for Area 31 (which encompasses all of lower Michigan and Northwest Ohio) remembered his work with Blight Busters some years back. A couple of phone calls later the corporate vice president was meeting with John in the Java Café. Perhaps a bit surreal, the Starbuck's VP was sipping a cup of Java Café's own "Ja Makin Me Crazy"! This marked the formation of a partnership that would bless this community in many ways over the years to come. While the National Conference never materialized for logistical reasons, the Starbucks Foundation was determined to find new ways to partner with the Motor City Blight Busters. In January the Michigan team with Marty Cook and his associates, met to discuss plans for the District Leadership Conference to be held in April. They made arrangements for the 250 plus participants to come out to volunteer with Motor City Blight Busters for one day of the conference.

Early Tuesday morning, April 9, 2012, with 30 mph winds blowing and overcast skies that would bring snow throughout the day, 100 Starbucks district managers from Illinois, Ohio, Indiana and Michigan along with another 150 partners (the term Starbucks uses to describe its employees) showed up to help with John's mission to "save the world, starting with Detroit."

What is it that endears people to one particular person? Some say it's charisma, that elusive quality that only a select group of people possess. Others might call it an allure or even something divine, but Marty summed it up best when he described his own attraction to John and the work he is doing. "John has a magnetic personality and that is what made me want to not only contribute personally to his mission but to get as many of my partners to contribute as well."

Magnetism - that is probably the best way to describe how John has been able to amass hundreds of partners through the years. People naturally gravitate toward John and within minutes they are drawn in and committed to help materialize the vision that John sets before them.

Most of the partnerships that John has formed began with individuals who saw his vision and returned to their company, group or organization so vitalized by John's positive energy that his magnetism actually works through them, connecting those with whom they share their story. That is truly one powerful magnet, or just maybe there is a little something divine about John's mission after all.

Volunteers

While partnerships provide the framework for the Motor City Blight Busters it is the volunteers that supply the true lifeblood of this organization. Blight Busters thrives on the work accomplished by its abundance of volunteers. Doctors, farmers, engineers, union workers, bartenders, high school students, college interns, families, churches, rich, poor, African-American, Jewish, Irish, Asian, Native American, All-American, retired, unemployed hearing impaired, wheelchair bound, small and frail or large and strong- all types of people from every background and walk of life have made their way to these humble grounds. They come with warm hearts eager to share their time. Some are strong, but many simply come with hands anxious to make a difference. Some are professional craftsmen bringing their equipment, tools and expertise, while many more are caring people with a willingness to do whatever is asked of them.

Each volunteer has an experience that is personal, unique and most often transforming. It is hard not to be changed after seeing how much a few hours of work has made an impact on this community. There are as many stories as there are volunteers - some seem to be almost carbon copies of each other, while others are as original and unique as the people themselves who are making these amazing contributions. Telling these many stories would take a book in itself, and may just be the follow-up to this one story. But for this book, the stories, praises and comments are woven throughout the manuscript to season the story with a personal perspective from the heart of everything happening on the site, in the field, on the stage and on the streets of the community John George is ushering back into life.

"It is a John George special!"
"Holy Moly!

Chazz Miller

Urban Warrior Photo Album

F
A
M

Mr. and Mrs. Dominic Conflitti, Virginia Conflitti George, Edmund George, Aunt Sayad George and Uncle Joe

I
L
Y

John William Anne Marie John Alicia and Jamal

John William and

Anne Marie

Lonnie, Alicia John and Ann Marie

The George Family: John, Robert, Edmund, Mike,
Diane Jacokes, Carol Kirkland and Virginia George

Todd McKler
And Ann Marie

Mama Gloria and
Lilliecrest

President Barack Obama & John   Vice President Joe Biden & John

John, Mayor Dave Bing, Alicia and Tom O'Brien

Governor Jennifer Granholm
& John

Mayor Dennis Archer & John

Alicia George

JAVA

HOUSE

Kofe Roval

Early Headquarters
remodeling

Virginia, John &
Alicia George

With 2013 VW Car
from Oprah

Editor, Faith Doody, CTR Summer Mission 2014
Glenn Doody, Tim Andridge, Sean Doody, Arron
Doody, Kevin Doody and Alan Doody

Chris Lambertsen & Frank Arce

Lauren Barber, Laura Kroll, Miriam Wisnewski & Amy Abramaczyk

Michelle Certain

CHRIST THE REDEEMER SUMMER MISSION

Dakarai Carter

Derrol Johnson

VOUNTEERS

The Making of a Village 8

I love coffee, I love tea
I love the java jive and it loves me
Coffee and tea and the java and me
A cup, a cup, a cup, a cup, a cup, boy

I love java, sweet and hot
Whoops, Mr. Moto, I'm a coffee pot
Shoot me the pot and I'll pour me a shot
A cup, a cup, a cup, a cup, a cup

The Ink Spots

John always had a vision of the downtown area becoming vibrant again. He could see people flowing in and out, a type of kinetic energy, with a feel of life and liveliness. He knew in his heart what this would one day be, but just how that was going to flush out, he wasn't quite sure. So he continued doing what he always did believing that the rest of the details would take care of themselves.

The evolution of the Village can be credited to the synergy of three dynamic people, Alicia Marion, Chazz Miller and of course, John George. Each person brought a personal dream that blended with a vision for the Village. Providence brought these three spirits together and their energy overflowed the small world of Old Redford until their visions converged to create a nexus of hope and community.

One cannot say that there was ever one specific moment that occurred where they joined forces but there was certainly a Power greater than them that set everything in motion.

The evolution of this dynamic trio began on a hot summer day in 1999, a typical work day for John - demolition, cleaning streets and picking up garbage - when he took his work crew into the legendary Laffrey's Steakhouse for a moment of relaxation and a break from the heat. Covered with the elements of the project, dirt, dust and a little bit of the indistinguishable - the crew walked in laughing and carrying on in a demeanor befitting a hard-working bunch, when they were met at the hostess stand by a beautiful lady who was new to the eatery. Greeting them with her stunning smile, Alicia was not sure how to proceed. She pleasantly excused herself and went to her manager who, by the way, uncanny as it is was, was named George. With a perplexed look Alicia said, "George, can they eat here? They're all dirty." Her manager was quick to respond warmly "Oh, that John George. He knocks down crack houses he can sit anywhere he wants to!" "That just sounds dangerous", thought Alicia to herself, "A man that smashes crack houses can come in here and sit down anywhere he wants to?!"

Alicia was initially reserved about her feelings for a man who got dirty on a daily basis and did a most unusual sort of work. She would greet him politely and engage in conversation when their paths crossed, but to say there was an attraction would be a stretch. However, their paths continued to cross and as destiny, fate or God had planned, John and Alicia would encounter each other again and again in the course of daily business. It was after the third or fourth chance encounter that Alicia said to herself, "I've got to check this place out and volunteer."

It was during just such an encounter at the Secretary of State's office that Alicia got to know John better. Alicia shares, "You know how you have to wait so long there? We were able to have a real conversation. We sat down and talked and he told me more details about his organization, the mission, the cause and the movement. He said, 'You need to come to the Community Center.' I said, 'You know I'm coming right now.' I went right from the Secretary of States to the Community Center. At that time the first floor was being used as a garage where cars were being worked on as part of a car donation program. The second floor was hardwood floors, absolutely gorgeous! And the third floor was a theater with a cathedral ceiling and winding staircase. That was it. I said, 'Okay, what's my part? I'm in!' And that's how it started!" Alicia laughs as she fondly remembers those early days.

Through the next few years Alicia and John formed a working relationship that was like a Fred Astaire and Ginger Rogers dance. They were in step; they felt each other's stir before the move and knew where to place the next step. Their graceful motion flowed through the unpredictable landscape of the business, creating a rhythm that swept the team along. In the beginning Alicia, offered to schedule the volunteers and prepare them for their workday, processing waivers and instructing the volunteers on what they would need to ensure a safe and meaningful experience. Gradually she moved into handling all the logistical and administrative aspects of the business.

As the Blight Busters vision was taking on new dimensions – flowing from the Community Center into the surrounding business district - the seeds for the coffeehouse that Alicia had always dreamed of were planted. Still working in a business relationship a couple of years after they had met, John looked at Alicia saying, "You know how I help everybody - so why shouldn't I help you? You're my assistant. I'll just keep my eye out for a building and we can turn it into a coffeehouse."

Alicia fondly recalls how they would explore the neighborhoods, sometimes riding their bikes. During their travels they finally found the perfect little place. "It was at Six Mile and Lahser, a coffeehouse with the same colors we now have in the Java House. Outside were the same shades of green and brown. It had four pillars painted different colors with a long porch and a parking lot to the side. It was perfect!" The reflection of that little place dances in Alicia's eyes as she tells the story. It was her dream, but before she had a chance to hang her sign and make it her own, the site caught fire and quickly became a drown dream. While the search continued for the next site Alicia kept herself busy. During the day she continued her administrative duties at the headquarters, and in the evenings and early morning hours she began moonlighting at Starbucks. If she couldn't have her own shop yet, she was determined to breathe in the aroma of the beans and build her dream as she learned everything there was to know about the coffee business.

Moving forward in time to the spring of 2003, an artist and philosopher of life, Chazz Miller, was letting life take him where it led. Chazz knew his life would always involve art but sometimes life gets in the way. Over recent years he had been painting commercially to pay the bills. One has to eat and take care of the bare necessities, so he was busy painting the new condos and developments that were being built in the suburbs. While work was plentiful and the money was very good he was realizing that he wasn't living his dream, that of painting art and living a life that would perpetuate his vision of creating an urban community centered around art. Chazz recalls, "So I said, 'I don't want to end up that old guy that could've been a great artist but now he is a painter.' I had a vision", screeching like squealing tires Chaz continues, "I put on the brakes, and I put it out in the universe, 'I want to paint murals'!"

At the time Chazz was working on a side project helping out a small charter school in Detroit, painting murals in the classrooms to liven up the walls. At the end of the project he crossed paths with an old friend who pointed him in the direction of another mural project at a different Detroit school. At the end of his work there he was cleaning his brushes when his phone rang and he was connected to another painting partner, "Chaz this is Martin, I'm at Blight Busters they need a mural like yesterday, they got Granholm coming,"

"It is a John George special!" Chazz recalls, "Holy Moly! So I just finished packing up my truck, and said, 'I'll be right over.'" So began the friendship and partnership between Chazz and John, a partnership that would change the corner of Lahser and Grand River forever.

Things moved rather quickly once these two passionate people joined forces. Chazz had written his vision for art in the community, about four years prior and had been waiting for the opportunity and the right person to introduce it to. After just a few conversations with John and completing that first project he knew this was the time and John was that person. Chazz shared with John his vision for an artist's community where people could gather to cultivate their art. It wouldn't be just an art studio for painters, but "for all forms of art, textile artists, woodcarvers, ceramic artists, painters, poets, musicians, all under one roof." Chazz's vision was of a place where artists could eat, gather, share and develop their talents in collaboration. This idea of art as a practice in community development was a model that Chazz was introduced to in Germany through the Bahá'í faith community. [ii]

The Bahá'í faith sees the relationship between art and spirituality as a culture that, when practiced "seeks to promote spiritual growth by ennobling and uplifting the individual soul and the collective life of humanity." [iii]

"The Bahá'í social ideal guarantees that artists, as individuals, can serve society without their initiative or creativity being stifled. This ideal involves "a social system at once progressive and peaceful, dynamic and harmonious, a system giving free play to individual creativity and initiative but based on co-operation and reciprocity."

The Village would eventually evolve around this philosophy and vision; but, it would take time, prayer, money, a lot of setbacks and just as many miracles before it would become a reality. Chazz had just finished a second mural, a garden mural on a business located at the corner of Six Mile and Lahser, and John called him. "Chazz, you're serious about this aren't you." Chazz was quick to respond, " I sure am." John continued, "I don't have money but I have walls and a lot of paint and manpower, what do you want to do?" Chazz responded, "Lets get to work."

And work they did, when Chazz wasn't painting murals on the downtown businesses he was busy painting large signs for the car donation program that John had launched. Chazz was working in his mother's small garage, he laughs as he describes the situation, "I had all these 4x8 pieces of plywood stacked in my mother's garage tryin to paint them. And I said, 'John I need a studio. You give me all this stuff and I love it, but literally, my mama's garage is down to an aisle way and a little wall I paint on. John you have all these vacant buildings and you can't find me nothing,? Come on you're John George!'

Things were about to change, Alicia recalls the day when

Doug Robertson, the owner of the vacant buildings between the theatre and the alley, came calling for a hand. In need help to preserve his own space on Lahser and Grand River, Doug was looking for someone who could create a presence and protect it from crime and theft.

Doug saw the work that Chazz had been doing and asked if he could paint a mural on the side of his building, a sign perhaps to send a message that there was a business and activity operating there. "He called John and said, 'Hey there are people dumping an the alley and I'm getting tickets for blight. I'm wondering if you could come over here and clean this up. Can you put a Blight Busters logo up here so people know it's you and they will quit doing it?

My first memory of the Java House was going into this building that was totally a mess and having Alicia and John talk about their vision of having a coffee house in this space - I couldn't see it but I was willing to believe it - watching the changes over the years and now seeing the final product, has given me hope for the area and I will never doubt John & Alicia when they have a vision.

Martha Jordan

After a walk through of the meandering buildings that comprised the Robertson property, John could see the possibilities. With that third eye of John's engaged, he was quickly describing the vision, a stage with local performers entertaining streams of people, a coffee shop with people gathering for conversation and poetry, enjoying local food and fresh brewed coffee. In another area would be a computer café and in another area gardens where fresh vegetables would be grown for the food in the coffee shop. It was a kaleidoscope of colors, people, art and hope. As they were walking through the building with Doug, assessing the property, Chazz remembers, "I elbowed John and said 'This is it. This is my studio right here." While, Alicia adds, "Then he said to me, 'Okay Alicia I think this right here would be perfect for your coffee shop!'" It was difficult for Alicia to see through John's eyes as she looked around at a collection of structures that were filled with filth, abandoned car parts, broken floors and a ceiling falling in. Chazz continues "It wasn't fit for humans, period. There was this much oil on the floor, (raising his hands to represent about 4 inches of oil) there were rats running everywhere, and one wall leaked bad." Alicia trying to restrain herself responded, "I was looking for something more like a house with a kitchen or something." But John wouldn't let her dismiss the idea "It'll be beautiful let's get it started." Within less then a year John had worked out an agreement with the Robertson family to provide security for the property while maintaining and improving the structures in return for a no-strings attached free lease. John recalls, "Over the course of the year we just phased it out. Phase 1 we did the floors, phase 2 we did the plumbing and so forth. I would say over 2001 and 2002 we completed the initial work and by 2003 all of our visions purged together into the Artist Village."

"When I come to this place I feel invited!"
Anonymous

"I feel a whole bunch of things. I fell inspiration, I feel desperation, I feel energy, . . . " Resurrection "A spiritual presence of joy."

The village grew around the Blight Buster deconstruction projects. As was John's habit, he began another dance, a dance with the village that was a minuet of sorts. Dips, sways and steps that marked movements of creation. When funding was more accessible building materials would be purchased and a small section would get some attention. Despite the erratic pattern to construction little impeded the energy of creation. In the early years summer jazz nights would be celebrated within the walls with little more than a couple old couches and the enthusiasm of passionate artists. Eager liked spirits would fill the space, bringing their own chairs or blankets to have a place to sit and be a part of an energy that they found hard to describe. As people came from near and far to find out for themselves what the magic was here, more money followed. In time a stage and an art gallery were added to the venue. The little bohemian theatre quickly became recognized by local artists and aficionados of urban art, gathering on Friday nights to be entertained by the musical speech of spoken word. The creative energy and musical rhythms ebbed into the early hours of the morning to continue on again after a brief break to allow for sleep. The following afternoon as the folks made their way back to the village a barbeque of chicken, hamburger, or maybe ribs would greet them. Another evening of entertainment would cascade the eclectic group into the early morning hours of Sunday.

Thus began a rhythm of music and a spirit of love and life that filled the corner of Lasher and Grand River creating an identity of its own.

At the same time, staying true to his vision of establishing a community center where an appreciation for art would be cultivated, Chazz created Detroit Public Art Works, P.A.W.S.. P.A.W.S. was an outreach initiative that incorporated teaching youngsters of the area painting skills woven with ideals of hope, wisdom and encouragement. They learned that indeed they were special and could hope for a future that was bright with possibility like the paints that they were applying to the blank canvas.

Ever so slowly, the coffee shop emerged. The energy and spirit that flowed through the village, the local businesses and the community merged together to where it funneled into the space that would become the coffee shop, creating the feel of a sacred space. If something could be willed into existence, it could be said that indeed that was the case with the Java House. People who heard John's story, saw his love for Alicia and experienced Alicia's love for believing in this dream, made a commitment to do what they could to help them both realize this dream. A dollar here and there, volunteer hands and networking with the people who could make it happen all joined together with the power of the Almighty to birth a dream and create a sanctuary where one could find peace, comfort, encouragement and hope. Java House today is a testament to what faith and fortitude can create with the power of believing that the impossible is possible.

I have known from a very young age, five or six, that I was sent here to do something out of the ordinary.

But I had no idea what it was until I boarded up that house.

That was when the Lord revealed to me what I should be doing.

Farm City

9

Where flowers bloom so does hope. -Lady Bird Johnson

On the corner of Rockdale and Midland, there lies a vacant lot that once held a bountiful garden that provided food for family and friends. John recalls, "This is the lot where my grandfather grew all the vegetables and fruit you could eat. During the summer we would come here and just eat out of the garden: fresh tomatoes, cucumbers, apples, grapes, plums, cherries, peaches, everything. It was great!" Perhaps this was where John's appreciation for organic and homegrown produce was nurtured. Before urban gardening became a coined term, and before the City began its blitz to transform the vacant landscape into huge gardens, John was humbly cultivating and planting the small lots he was turning over into green spaces for the neighbors to grow vegetables for their families. It wasn't any monumental plan, it was simply putting seeds in the ground and feeding the people.

Over the past 10 years urban gardening has grown in Detroit and has been on the lips of who want to grab onto something positive that is thriving in the City. Urban gardening is not new to Detroit or other large cities. As America has had to rediscover itself and move from manufacturing to other avenues of revenue, cities have repurposed vacated ground that is ripe for planting. At the same time, the sustainable farming movement fits perfectly in the wave to reinvent the urban landscape. Opportunities for young, budding farmers are abundant, whether it is the college student who has an apartment off of the Woodward corridor and wishes to experiment with a few tomato and lettuce plants, or the neighborhood gardener who makes use of the vacant lot next door. People are rediscovering the art of small plot farming. There are many benefits -

not just for the City - in reclaiming the land, but for the farmer, the neighborhood and the preservation of community.

The practice of reassigning city lots for farm use is not a new one. Back in the late 1800s Hazen Pingree, Detroit's progressive mayor, "suggested the creation of urban gardens to give the unemployed and their families something useful to do. These garden plots became known as Pingree Potato Patches." The concept of urban gardening did as much for the self-confidence and personal wellbeing of the unemployed worker as it did to feed the families suffering through the depressed economic conditions they were facing. The concept was so popular that within a year, it was spreading to other major cities throughout the country. (Gallaher)

Today the city of Detroit is the home to many community gardens throughout its neighborhoods. The Capuchin Brothers support one of these gardens, known as Earthworks. Not only does it supplement their Soup Kitchen, but it also serves as a training and education center for such skills as beekeeping and mulching. Begun in the late 1990s the project's mission was to "restore our connection to the environment and community."

It is this concept of justice in food distribution that has spurred on the community garden movement. Food desert, a term that has become synonymous with the city and the inequity of food distribution, fuels the movement in urban gardening. Historically, food distribution in the early part of the 20th century came from the neighborhood stores. These quaint little grocers were located right in the center of a block of homes. They were easily accessible for all families, with stores dotted throughout the neighborhoods. These family-owned shops offered personal service and access to fresh meats and vegetables that came from local farmers or the farmers market.

These mom and pop shops disappeared for the most part during the 1960s when civil unrest threatened the owners and their businesses. Families moved out to the new, expanding suburbs and the local grocery stores were abandoned. Today families depend on convenience stores attached to gas stations and the handful of independent grocers that still exist in the City. There is nothing left within walking distance or even close enough for a short car ride. Families must drive outside the city limits to grocery chain stores like Meijer, Kroger or other independent stores that provide fresh food.

"Roughly 550,000 Detroit residents – over half of the City's total population – live in areas that are far out-of-balance in terms of day-to-day food availability. This means that they must travel twice as far or farther to reach the closest mainstream grocer as they do to reach the closest fringe food location, such as a fast food restaurant or a convenience store." (Gallagher)

A study by LaSalle Bank, *Examining the Impact of Food Deserts on Public Health in Detroit*, made it clear that the lack of healthy food options leads to "food imbalance, a serious public health concern, and will likely have compounded effects on Detroit and the region unless access to healthy food greatly improves." Research has produced "evidence that communities with food imbalance are more likely to experience worse diet-related health outcomes than other communities, even when those communities have similar socio-economic characteristics.

The types of food options we live closest to – along with many other factors – are related to our health." (Gallagher)

Knowing the facts does little if there is no effort to change the system. John has understood this from day one. Cleaning the streets and removing blight is only the beginning. To create a thriving community, there must be an infrastructure that can provide healthy food choices, good schools, and local business and job opportunities that can support families. While the plan is evolving slowly, John saw the importance of fresh grown food from the beginning, planting the first garden in 2003 on the side of a business. He followed that up with the garden within Artist's Village in 2005, situated within a small alcove between buildings. The brick walls made it a quaint European-type garden that is very common in city dwellings. First the walls were transformed, with young volunteers painting colorful pictures of fruits and vegetables in graffiti style. Next, clean rich soil was brought in and then the seeds were planted. A beautiful garden of mixed greens, tomatoes, beans, herbs and peppers has become an annual tradition since then.

(Detroit Free Press April 9th, 2012)

"It started on Orchard Street and then we took over some other lots farther over and created a melon farm with cantaloupe and watermelon, and got the people in the community involved," Kofi Royal shares. Kofi has been the resident "Master Gardener" for Blight Busters for the past several years and has overseen the expansion of the garden program from within the walls of Artist Village and out into the community. When Kofi saw how the vacant lots were being turned into dumping grounds - with people throwing garbage, furniture, tires, along with anything and everything because it was open space - he decided it was time to turn these lots into true green spaces, with trees, plants and food for the community.

But Kofi's vision is bigger than that. "My vision is to create a permaculture environment. That is, basically permanent agriculture - a totally natural setting with trees, fruit trees, bushes, animals and vegetables in an interrelated ecological growing environment that doesn't require the kind of maintenance that traditional farming requires. You use the natural surroundings and grow within the confines of that environment."

What Kofi is talking about is not new: in fact, it has its roots in the early part of the 20th century. The term permanent agriculture was actually introduced by Franklin Hiram King in his classic book of 1911, *Farmers of Forty Centuries: Or Permanent Agriculture in China, Korea and Japan.* Hiram introduced the idea of sustainable farming long before corporate farms would take over the agriculture industry.

There were many other influences through the decades, but the idea of sustainable farming further rooted itself in the 1970s and gained momentum through the 80s & 90s. Permaculture design emphasizes the interconnectedness of all living matter and, in some variations, also includes a social connectedness. In the 1970s two Australian farmers - Bill Mollison and David Holmgren - concerned with the overuse of non-renewable resources in industrial agriculture, set upon a path that would protect the land and animal life, while supporting a thriving biodiversity. This path became known as the design approach called "permaculture," and in 1978 they wrote and published

"Permaculture: a Designers Manual." In the manual, Mollison describes this interconnectedness as a belief "in caring for the Earth, our People, in balance and fair share. The only ethical decision is to take responsibility for our own existence and that of our children." Thus, the synergy that is created through the permaculture design brings not only a richness to the soil and its fruit, but creates a balance between man and the environment. All life is working together to enhance each other. (Mollison, The Permaculture Practitioner's Journal I, 1988) (Mollison, 1988)

Using the permaculture model, Kofi describes one of these methods in place in the community gardens, the "no-digging" approach; "In a permaculture situation the soil is hidden up underneath the natural composting that occurs when you just cut growth and lay it back down on the ground. That keeps the moisture right in the ground. I can plant cabbage and everything right there around those weeds. They are not really weeds they are part of the ecology." This practice produces a much "healthier" plant and food product.

It is interesting to note here, that while Kofi has been working to create this synergy within the community from the garden Chazz has had this same vision for the community through his work with the artists. Following the principals of the Bahá'í faith which sees the relationship between art and spirituality as a culture that, when practiced "seeks to promote spiritual growth by ennobling and uplifting the individual soul and the collective life of humanity," Chazz has encouraged the various art forms to work as one and create an all encompassing art life. An art life not only in media form but in lifestyle as all the artists work, live and socialize together. This vision in its most natural form occurs each day in the Java House as the artists flow in, through and out, are a part of the texture of the café. The energy that expands from this rhythm encompasses not just the café but this whole business district and community.

With gardens in the back of the Village lot and down Orchard Street and dotted throughout the five square mile district, there is a growing awareness of the importance of fresh food and an opportunity for the community to take part in reviving their own community.

Looking ahead, the Motor City Blight Buster 3-Year Master Plan calls for the expansion of the current garden located on Santa Clara "into an urban farm that will eventually span an entire city block. Working with partners at Fertile Ground Collective the plan is to cultivate this area and expand the community garden into an urban farm." The scope of the project is all encompassing to even include employing the help of neighbors and residents in the area "to help maintain a self-sufficient operation that everyone can participate in and enjoy."

While the gardens will surely provide some healthy food choices in the summer months it will take more than community gardens to provide families with wholesome food throughout the year. It is plans like the development of Meijer's that will bring a large variety of fresh food options year round for the local families along with the urban gardens that are creating the building blocks for healthy food choices for this community. "It only took 25 years but Rome wasn't built in a day." John shares as he enjoys a homemade soup in the Java Café.

10

BELIEVER

W Psalm 23

1The LORD is my shepherd, I shall not want. 2He makes me lie down in green pastures; He leads me beside quiet waters. 3He restores my soul; He guides me in the paths of righteousness For His name's sake. 4Even though I walk through the valley of the shadow of death, I fear no evil, for You are with me; Your rod and Your staff, they comfort me. 5You prepare a table before me in the presence of my enemies; You have anointed my head with oil; My cup overflows. 6Surely goodness and loving-kindness will follow me all the days of my life,
And I will dwell in the house of the LORD forever.

Looking around the coffee shop, John feels a sense of accomplishment. As his gaze turns to the window, it's as if there is an inaudible sigh - something he very seldom utters - but it flashes across his face. He continues on with his story almost without a breath:

"All we can do is continue to be optimistic, which is so important. It is really the only thing. If I had to pick one thing out of all the things that have kept us going, being optimistic is certainly A1. Optimism is kind of like faith and faith is so important. I will tell you why." Here John uses his hands to draw an imaginary line on the table. "If you are an optimist and don't have faith, let's say you stop here." He points to an imaginary line that he has drawn with his finger. "But your blessing is right there." He points to a spot about a foot past his line. "You gave up, you quit, you turned around, you went back and you never were there to claim that blessing, that resource, that victory, whatever it was. No matter how dark it gets - if you quit and turn around, you are not going to know what is on the other side of that curtain. That is why faith, is being optimistic. In my mind they go hand in hand. One kind of nudges the other and you see how things work out. We are still at it, 25 years later, and we are still as broke as a joke. But we have a nice coffee house. "

That is the how John has led his life from one moment to the next, relying on an unshakable trust, faith, and optimism that few can ever fully achieve. Anyone who has spent an afternoon with John probably never realized the weight he was carrying on his shoulders because he is so determined to be upbeat and emit positive energy to others.

Perhaps that is the key to his success in this little hamlet. Maybe it isn't the renovations, the new businesses that he boasts about, or the development of a dynamic artist's community. Maybe he has turned a whole community around by instilling a sense of faith, hope and optimism, a kinetic energy that is hard to shake when everyone is encouraging, supportive and smiling!

It is rare that John will open up and share his tragedies, but they are there - a current that runs far beneath his warm and faith-filled exterior. During the Winter of 2010, things were very dismal for Blight Busters. Despite John's determination and resounding optimism, one of the cornerstones of Blight Busters was lost. The Masonic Temple that had become the headquarters for the non-profit business had met its final, insurmountable challenge, with a loan that could not be paid. Blight Busters vacated the building, turning it back over to the bank.

Anyone who has been by the Village since July, 2012 knows that the building not only belongs to Blight Busters once again but it has been renovated and is now a fully operational Community Resource Center and Banquet Facility. It was more than John's determination and unrelenting will that made this possible, God was working through John and guiding him, and the Holy Spirit gave him inspiration, hope and wisdom to put each of the important pieces in place to make this a reality.

This is all part of John's spirituality. Raised in a Catholic home, going to Mass every Sunday "was a given; there was no choice," John's sister Carol Kirkland shares. John and his siblings not only attended Catholic grade school for eight years, but each of the six children also attended Catholic high schools. John attended St. Monica's until the sixth grade when the school closed, then finished out his elementary years at St. Christine's. John's education continued with four years at the newly opened Bishop Borgess High School located at the southend of Redford Township. It is no doubt that this Catholic education built a strong foundation for John's belief. Today, John may not be part of a traditional "organized religion, but he certainly has a personal relationship with God." (Kirkland C. , 2012)

Spirituality is a difficult concept to put into words. Each person defines it in how it applies to their own life. In John's life the Spirit fills his heart and each day guides him to change the world around him to make life a little better for others. Pope John Paul II said "If we live by the Spirit, let us also walk by the Spirit."[157] That is John! He literally walks the Holy Spirit, shaking hands, smiling, listening to other's hurts and struggles and then from his pocket, his heart and his back he gives what he can to help his brother and sister.

Martin Luther King, Jr. said, "God can speak directly with people in astonishingly personal ways." Truly John hears that voice of God everyday in his own life as he sets in motion a new project, a new venture and takes that leap of faith needed to make the plans come together.

Fr. James Martin in his account of Ignatius describes a God of surprise "who waits for us with wonderful things." And as John described in his own wisdom of optimism, one must never give up, for just the other side of the challenge and the obstacle of life there is a blessing, 'a wonderful thing.' It is this kind of faith that carries John through each of the crises that has beset him. This internal belief and faith, allows him to keep his head up and persevere whatever the odds. God is not the only one with surprises up his sleeve, John has provided many surprises as well, from finding a home for the homeless with but a nickel in his pocket and a prayer, to pulling off the feat of transforming a rundown, rat-infested building into a lively inspiring coffee house.

According to Deepak Chopra in the *Seven Spiritual Laws of Success.* (Chopra, 1993) "When we realize that our true Self is one of pure potentiality, we align with the power that manifests everything in the universe." It seems that John, through his unrelenting determination to make things right in his community and world, has unleashed his potentiality to accomplish good. Chopra explains it this way, "When you discover your essential nature and know who you really are, in that knowing itself is the ability to fulfill any dream you have, because you are the eternal possibility, the immeasurable potential of all that was, is and will be."

In the beginning, John simply had a need to keep his family safe and healthy, but out of that grew something bigger, a dream that was born out of this consciousness. A consciousness that he developed from a very young age, that was nurtured by a family who saw neighbors and community as an extension of their own family. A consciousness that understands the spiritual connection we have to one another - that what we do for another ultimately feeds our own soul as the energy flows from one to another and back again.

As Chopra so eloquently shares, "The universe operates through dynamic exchange . . . giving and receiving are different aspects of the flow of energy in the universe. *And it is our willingness to give that which we see, we keep the abundance of the universe circulating in our lives."* Everyday John gives back to the universe in a very profound way, conscious or unconscious. People from near and far see him work hard to make a change in the community by sweeping the streets, tearing down buildings, picking up garbage, organizing community projects, and much more. But few people ever see when he gives his coat to a homeless man who is cold, gives his partner money to fix his teeth or gives the man he just met his boots because the other man's feet are wet and cold from the holes in his own tattered shoes. What most people never see or know is when, without a meal himself, John gives his last dollar to the man on the corner who has not eaten in days, or when he walks everywhere because he has pawned his truck one more time to buy one more dumpster.

To conclude, John's unrelenting perseverance to do what is right comes from a deep faith and a belief that we are all connected, and whenever he changes the future for one person into something better he is impacting the world and making a better place for all.

11

URBAN WARRIOR

Fighting Injustice

Mother, mother
There's too many of you crying
Brother, brother, brother
There's far too many of you dying
You know we've got to find a way
To bring some lovin' here today - Ya

Father, father
We don't need to escalate
You see, war is not the answer
For only love can conquer hate
You know we've got to find a way
To bring some lovin' here today

Picket lines and picket signs
Don't punish me with brutality
Talk to me, so you can see
Oh, what's going on
What's going on
Ya, what's going on
Ah, what's going on

What's Going On, Marvin Gaye 1971

Injustice wears a lot of hats. It raises its head most often, though, where people are victims of circumstances beyond their control: oppression, famine, poverty, homelessness, and inequality. These people spend each waking hour attempting to meet basic human needs in an effort to survive. It is the greed of a few who make life seem hopeless for many. Injustice never makes sense, and while many wish to sincerely combat injustice, the road is complex and challenging, and often charged with "negative energy".

The injustice found in Brightmoor began over 80 years ago with the hopes and dreams of a group of people looking to make a better life for their families. It was not the intent of any person or group of people. Instead, it was the result of a series of events attributed to the rise of the Industrial Revolution rooted here in Detroit – the rise of the automobile, the creation of the assembly line, and the unprecedented increase in population without an infrastructure to support it.

In January, 1914 Henry Ford announced "a new profit-sharing plan that would boost workers' pay to $5 for an eight-hour workday. That was more than double the $2.25 he had been paying for a nine-hour day." (Company, Anniversary Souvenir) Young people from the southern states, seeking the greener pastures here in Michigan, saw the $5 work day as a golden egg. They packed up their few belongings and headed to Detroit with high expectations. Little did they realize, that finding a job was easier than finding a house.

The local housing market couldn't keep up with the sudden growth. In addition, Ford's new program had a few strings attached to it. "To qualify for the program and the job, workers had to allow representatives from Ford's new Sociological Department to inspect their homes to ensure the workers and their families were living clean lives of frugality and sobriety." A savvy investor and land developer, Burt Eddy Taylor (a.k.a. B. E. Taylor), offered these blindsided folks an answer. Buying up 160 acres of farmland, Taylor created one of the first subdivisions in Brightmoor. He also launched a real estate promotion that offered the eager homeowners a lot ready for building without any restrictions, so homeowners could erect whatever they wanted.

"As a result tents, tar paper shacks and some garage homes sprung up . . . There were no sanitary provisions, . . . no sewers, no electricity, gas or water."[1] While the new transplants' housing arrangements were less than adequate, they certainly met the terms of "frugality." [iv] (Carey, 1938) (Martelle, Detroit, A Biography)

Meanwhile, other subdivisions being built by competing developers in the Brightmoor area, didn't exhibit the poor conditions of the Taylor Company homes. Even so, these small, single-story frame houses were being thrown together as fast as possible. Many were completed within a week's time. These four-five room houses, were without basements, and the majority rested on wood pilings created from railroad ties.

Clearly this was a venture set up for failure. Fifteen years after the first lot was sold, Raymond Foley, the State Director of the Federal Housing Administration observed that this haphazard type of development was "physically and socially sick and a potential slum." How prophetic of this governmental leader; not only did Brightmoor become a slum in the early '30s but slum conditions persisted for the next eight decades, and the fight to redevelop this area continues to this day.

Surprisingly, many of these homes still stand today, and comprising a segment of the abandoned properties that Blight Busters work to remove as they continue to focus on fighting this injustice that began decades ago.

While the Brightmoor area would see improvements over the decades, this seemed to have become a battle that

would never end.   John was born in this corner of the
world on the east edge of Brightmoor. Perhaps his passion
for justice was sparked by watching his neighborhood and
City lose its life and its promise, one house at a time.

Growing up in the '60s and '70s, John - though too young
to fully comprehend the riots as they unfolded in 1967 -
still felt the impact and the aftermath of those turbulent
times of civil unrest.   In Michigan, forced bussing gave
way to resentment on both sides of the fence.   Children,
did not deserve to be used as pawns in this elaborate game
of politics, social justice and economics, were forced to
attend   schools   in   unfamiliar   and   sometimes   hostile
neighborhoods, leaving their friends and family miles away.
Many of them road the school bus thirty minutes or more
each   way   all   for   the   sake   of   forced   integration.
(Desegregation, a term used to put a more politically
correct spin on the process.)   Some families moved closer
to the school in an attempt to help their children, only to
endure attacks and resentment from right next door.   In
John's neighborhood, there were two African-American
families who moved in - the Holmes and the McKlers.

True   to   human   nature,   mistrust   and   uneasiness
accompanied the "neighborhood changing," to use the
words of the time.   It would take someone with charisma,
respect   and   an   open   mind   to   bring   the   new   mixed
community together.   Todd McKler shares; "John had a

lot to do with that. John was the guy who broke the ice in the neighborhood for a lot of people. He stuck his hand out to talk to people, to do whatever."

In his efforts to unite the home front, John recalls a day when he stepped in to put a stop to what he thought could become "the first race riot:"

In my family we were always taught to treat everyone the same. It didn't matter if they were rich or poor, black or white - we treated everyone with respect. I don't know what started the argument that day. I don't know how it came to a head. All I know is two people whom I considered to be my friends were threatening to kill each other.

That afternoon we were all playing baseball at the Saint Monica's baseball field. It was Todd McKler and Reggie Holmes - the two new black kids in the neighborhood - along with the Georges and several other white kids. I'm not sure exactly how it started; I just remember that there was some kind of disturbance. I remember Todd saying, "Get the walking tall. Get the walking tall." He was referring to a movie called "Walking Tall" (1973) where the main character carried a large stick as he cleaned up the town. I don't recall if they got the stick - but what I do remember is that I got between the one white guy and his family and Todd and his family and I got them to take it down a notch, basically diffusing it. I just remember that it was getting really ugly, really quick and my gut reaction was to get in-between

*because I was friends with both parties. It was subtle
diplomacy at its best. I don't know what happened to that
white guy but Todd and Reggie are still best friends of mine to
this day.*

"John was just that guy. John was probably before his
time. He was just a kid but he was almost a grownup,"
Todd McKler shares. It was in his blood, his nature.
From his early years he saw everyone with a sense that are
all equal, all are due respect and consideration. As John
likes to put it, "I guess I've always been for the underdog."
He lifts each person up and affirms who they are. John
gives everyone recognition for their contributions, praising
their efforts and talents without judgment. Dennis Archer
said it this way, "John is color blind. He is a remarkable
person who could very easily be a disciple of Dr. Martin
Luther King, in terms of how he treats the people around
him." (Archer, May) (McKler, 2012)

John's sense of justice is woven through and through. It is
not just second nature, it is his soul and essence. So why
does John tear down the abandoned homes and buildings?
"I live here on this street. I have a moral obligation to my
children, the other children who live here, and to the
seniors, to do what I think is right. It was Martin Luther
King, Jr. who said, 'You have a moral responsibility to
stand up to unjust laws.' To allow vacant, firebombed
wrecks to fester next to our children, our seniors, our

businesses, our community, is wrong. It is unjust."

This sense of justice and doing what is right that drives John, that gives him an endurance that few others will ever experience. John said he would work a million years - if he had a million years - to do this work. Listening to him and watching as he swings the ax again and again, it's easy to believe that he might just do it.

John reflects on his calling to this mission:

> *I have known from a very young age, five or six, that I was sent here to do something out of the ordinary. But I had no idea what it was until I boarded up that house. That was when the Lord revealed to me what I should be doing.*

12
SMOKE AND MIRRORS
"And when the smoke clears, everything that I promised is there."
John George, 2012

"Knowledge kills action;
action requires the veils of illusion."
Friedrich Nietzsche

An illusion, deception, trickery. Smoke and mirrors - a phrase associated with not only mystery, but a con. It's an odd term to use in the conversation about a man who has done so much for his community, yet a term that was actually presented by John to describe himself. So what is behind the smoke and mirrors? What is the illusion that John creates?

It is easy to get caught up in the illusion created by the Village itself - where the vibrant Java House and stately Redford Theatre are the anchors for the business community. Surrounding them are more businesses that have either held their own through troubling times, or are new attempts to foster a livelihood on a dream and a prayer.

The backdrop of murals and a flow of creative souls create the smoke and mirrors illusion of an Artists hamlet. In fact, while meandering through the maze behind the coffee shop on a Saturday night, patrons and passersby feel that they are in a quaint artists' colony, reminiscent of the bohemian lifestyle of the'70s. And perhaps therein lies the smoke and mirrors.

Surrounding this little sanctuary are buildings in various stages of decay. Homes just a block over are crumbling. Once friendly neighborhoods with children playing contentedly are now empty and foreboding. Yet, music bursts forth from Artist Village, infusing life while sirens blare outside the walls - another life taken, another bit of hope extinguished, another illusion of what is and isn't. Is this an artists' community or a city of despair?

When John meets someone for the first time, he takes them to the site where he is working and tells the story of how he got to this place. He quickly segues into the story of what will come next. With his charisma and passion, he paints a picture that the mind is eager to embrace. "This will become a community garden. After you remove the negative energy, we will bring in clean topsoil. We will put a fence around it and create a garden of vegetables and fruit for the neighbors. Next spring you will see lettuce, tomatoes, greens, carrots and squash. The neighbors will come out and have picnics here. Children will play here and all the folks will help maintain the green space. In the fall we will have a barbeque and celebrate with music, spoken word and some good fresh food. Be sure to come back and join us."

John's audience is mesmerized and the smoke and mirrors have begun. Yes it is an illusion - but it is not a deception or con. It is a masterful manipulation of the truth. John has a unique gift for making unbelievers believe in the impossible. As John will say, "Nothing is impossible." He so believes that to be true that he wills the impossible to become the possible. As he so eloquently describes, "When the smoke clears, everything that I promised is there in concrete form - you can touch it, feel it."

Kevin Johnson, John's long-time friend and loyal right-hand-man tells this story: "The building (that was to become the headquarters) was a total dump when I first saw it. The windows were all broken out; the roof was gone; pigeons were flying around; bird feces, dead birds and trash were everywhere. We would use kerosene heaters when we were working just to keep warm. A lot of people tried to take that building on and do something with it, but they all gave up. When he had no money at all, he still had drive. He'd say 'I've got to get this done I've got to get this done.'"

In those first few months when the grim process of cleaning out the facility was in its earliest stages, John had placed his large oak desk prominently in a back room of the second floor. The solid oak floor was still warped and uneven from years of neglect. Kevin recalls, "We would sit there at night, sometimes with a drink, and he would dream. John would say, 'I'm going to have French doors right here.' He described it to a tee, the way it is today. There was no furnace, no plumbing, no electricity. We were sitting there in candlelight with our coats on, shivering, and he said this is the way it is going to be."

Years later - after investing 1.4 million dollars in renovations and reconstruction - Kevin and John were sitting in that same spot. Kevin continues, "He was sitting behind that same desk and I was sitting on the other side and I said 'John, it is just like you said at the very beginning. You were sitting right there where you are now when you described exactly this.' John responded, with a chuckle in his voice, "Yes, isn't it amazing?"

"And when the smoke clears, everything that I promised is there."

John explains, "What I mean by smoke and mirrors is how we get from point A to point B, and it might not be the most graceful thing you've ever seen." This could not be any more true than when it comes to tearing down abandoned buildings. Ideally, the project begins with a permit, turning off the utilities and prepping the site. However, Kevin Johnson recalls a time when they first began the demolition process: "Two busloads of volunteers had pulled up. I said to John, 'I didn't know we had all these volunteers coming in today.' John wasn't aware either. I asked, 'John, what are we going to do?' He points to a firebombed house across the street saying, 'We're going to take that house down right there.' We didn't have a permit or anything. And we didn't have a dumpster.

What are you going to do? You hate to disappoint the volunteers; you know this is what they want to do. They want some demolition. So we started picking it apart and it wasn't long before the City Inspector showed up and gave us a ticket. John says, 'We'll take the ticket, but we're not going to stop. We are going to tear the house down, right now.' "

John is quick to explain that this was in the past. Now everything is done by the books, "We don't have to do it illegally anymore; we can do it legally. In the past, the truth is that we tore things down without permits. Now, moving forward, we're going to cross the t's and dot the i's and do what we can to follow the proper way. I can assure you that as we move into the future, we will not dismantle or deconstruct or demolish any properties in

Detroit without a permit."

Revitalizing Detroit over the past 25 years has been a monstrous task and a roller coaster ride. John lost his house to foreclosure in 2010, and spent 2011 moving from place to place - sometimes sleeping in one of the Blight Busters properties. During this time, the Motor City Blight Busters headquarters building was also foreclosed. None of it has been easy, but according to John's well-known philosophy, "If it was easy everybody would be doing it." John perseveres.

John lives in the moment. In a single motion, he might give his coat to a stranger and then walk over to an abandoned house to begin knocking it down with his bare hands. John doesn't wait for an invitation (or, for that matter, permission.) This cavalier attitude can sometimes cause setbacks when it is taken offensively by others. This is the smoke that has occasionally clouded the mirror in the past. For those who are not in the loop, who are not part of the Blight Busters circle, seeing John pull down a garage with a rope tied to his front bumper might look like vandalism. Emptying an abandoned home throwing its contents into a dumpster or onto the berm where passers-by pick through may seem questionable.

John agrees he's taken a few missteps along the way; "I've made mistakes, absolutely. If I could change some things, I definitely would. Have I ever purposely plotted to steal something from someone, or do something, illegal? Absolutely not. I believe I have a moral obligation to my children, my family and my community to protect them from what's outside there. If there is a crack house at the end of my block that my children can look at when we are eating dinner and the City is not going to do what they are chartered to do, then I'm going to do it. Twenty-Five years later, I have figured out a process so I can do it legally and actually make a profit." The smoke clears once more.

John defines his life by dividing it into two realms: corporate life and personal life. While it may seem humanly impossible for John to have a personal life, he does a dance that weaves the two together, at times a little precariously. More smoke and mirrors.

Ann Alexander, John's first wife, recalls the early years of their marriage as being "turbulent." With much affection for John, she reflects on when things began to change. As John's passion for driving out the drug dealers began to set in, he took what had started as a weekend mission and made it a full-time project around 1993.

"I was very frightened when John came home and said, 'I sold my book of business. I'm done and I want to go in a new direction now.' [v] I was very concerned how we were going to support ourselves and our kids in this house. It was very scary for awhile because it was not a money-producing thing. Even though John made money selling his book of business, I knew it wasn't going to last. So I was very concerned about how we were going to make ends meet."

"It was a raw spot; it was very difficult. If I knew then what I know now, maybe I would have been able to adjust to it more easily. But I was a newlywed with little kids and I'm thinking, 'What is he doing?'

"That was the biggest thing tearing us apart, the uncertainty. There was no money coming in. In the early days he was spending what we had. At that time he would spend our money purchasing items for other people, or for the neighborhood. It was an honorable thing, but at the time I was thinking about our children."

In 1994 John and Ann legally divorced and parted ways. While they had separate homes and lives, their children remained first place in both of their hearts. Ann finished school and became a counselor, providing a safe and secure home and establishing herself in a career that embraced a mission of compassion that seemed to envelope the lives of John William and Ann Marie. "My kids have benefited tremendously by the way they've grown up. They have big hearts and they believe in hard work and community," Ann shares. (Interview, 2012)

A few years later, John met Monica White, someone who filled an emptiness he felt, but their relationship wasn't destine to last. John recalls, "I met Monica at a gas station. We were having one of our party functions and I think I may have given her a flyer. Monica showed up at the party and it kind of snow balled from there." They were married in October 1997 but divorced just three years later. (George J. , October 2012, 2012)

In the summer of 1999, John met Alicia Marion - not at a nightclub or a party - but at the restaurant where he would bring his workers for a treat after a long day. Thus began the dance that would waltz through winds of change and storms of disaster and crescendo with the wedding dance.

After their third random encounter, moved by John's mission and enthusiasm, Alicia jumped in as a volunteer herself. "I would help when the volunteers arrived - greeting them, having them sign waivers and handing out masks and gloves. Later, I worked assisting John with call backs, checking messages, looking up resources, acting as an office assistant." By the time the organization moved into the main headquarters, Alicia was juggling all of it - running the accounting department, organizing the volunteers, overseeing the car donation program, writing press releases and coordinating fundraising and community events. As Alicia puts it, "It was strictly business." (Marion, 2012)

The turn of the millennium was a milestone in both of their lives. In the spring of that year, John had a meeting that took him out of town for several days and Alicia was running the whole show. When he left town she was confident she could run the business and manage on her own. A strong, smart and independent woman, Alicia proved that indeed she could run the business, solve any problem and make the necessary decisions without hesitation. What she didn't expect was how much she missed John - not for his leadership, but for the companionship, friendship and relationship that was budding between them. "He had given me everything to take care of while he was gone. When he came back I confessed, 'Oh my God, I missed you, and he replied, 'Didn't you know that absence makes the heart grow fonder?' That was when I knew it was him. That is when we officially became a couple." (Marion, 2012)

While business kept the relationship on a professional level, a spark that ignited in John when he first met Alicia and grew into a flame as the passion of John's mission became as much a part of Alicia's life as it was John's. When they weren't working, they were being pulled together just the same by their sons. Jamal, Alicia's only child, was just a couple of years younger than John William and the two struck up a friendship which quickly became true kinship. They would spend weekends together, and when Alicia wasn't shuttling them to an activity John would step in to take up the task. Having picnics and evening dinners together was the norm, and trips to get ice cream were not uncommon.

Even with this much time together over a two-year period, John and Alicia still had not been on an actual date. It wasn't until the night John came home from that business trip that everything changed. As he remembers, "Our first official date was when I got back from working out of town. I was in Washington working with Massco and somehow when I got back, either I called her or she called me and she said she was going to be at a restaurant/club in the area. So when I got back into town I stopped by. She was there with a girlfriend. Her girlfriend ended up leaving and I drove Alicia home. That was the first time I kissed her and she started crying. I think she was crying because she had feelings for me and they had bubbled to the surface. I would say that was when it went from strictly business to a personal relationship."

John is quick to declare that he is "madly in love with Alicia." Spending one minute with the two of them together in a room makes this crystal clear. John found a love that was deep and true in Alicia. It is the kind of love that comes after experiencing loss, hurt and deep pain. It is a mature love that can only develop after many life experiences; a love that isn't just about two people, but how they change the world into something better because the two of them are one. That is what John found in Alicia, their love wasn't founded on fun times or heated passion that erupted between them, but a passion that flowed through both to entwine into a single burning desire to help others.

John was quick to recognize this in Alicia when she first came to Blight Busters as a volunteer. The organization had just joined forces with the Heat and Warmth Fund (THAW) and was helping local families prepare paperwork and get access to funding so they could have heat. Alicia saw each homeowner for the person that he or she was. She would sit with them, compassionately hearing their stories and reaching out to them lovingly - often times not just helping them with THAW but connecting them with other resources that they needed to survive. It was this compassion that drew John in, and it was this love within Alicia that melted John's own heart.

It is people like John and Alicia who make this world such a wonderful place to live. They give endlessly of themselves - working tirelessly to help others, bring justice and make the impossible possible. There is not a clock to be found around the building or the Village because time has no beginning or end when your mission is helping others. Needs arise at any time, day or night, and often in the middle of the night. There are no holidays or weekends off in the fight against negative energy and the building of goodwill.

Needless to say, John and Alicia were working nonstop, day in and day out, 24-7. This can wear on any person, and for a young couple in love it leaves little time to be alone together. They found they needed to escape from the Village for a weekend to truly spend time together. No phones, pagers or people dropping by. "We vacationed in Detroit more than once. We would go downtown for a couple of days and stay at one of the hotels," John recalls.

Such a brutal schedule is hard on the best of relationships and it was no different for John and Alicia. In the beginning, the weekend getaway every few months would be enough to bring the spark back, but after time this wasn't enough. The phone calls and constant demands on John's attention were enough to pull him away Alicia. Alicia was ready for a permanent relationship where she could share private time with John and not have to share herself with a business that would show no mercy.

It was late 2009 when the tides of discontent were too strong to keep the relationship intact. John recalls, "It was because of a lot of stress - the foreclosure on the house, losing the building - just anything that you can imagine that can tear people apart."

John was not about to let this woman of compassion, the love of his life, the "person who made him feel at home," go. John shares, "I realized how much I loved her and missed her. I promised to do some things differently as far as setting limits around how many hours I would work and how many projects I would be involved in." And then he wooed her with flowers, dinners and giving her the time and attention that was befitting this woman he loved with such depth.

Reuniting was just the first step. There were other hurdles to overcome in making the relationship permanent. In the fall of 2011 John sighed, "We have been so consumed with what I am doing, what she is doing and what we are doing together, that we don't even have time to plan our own wedding. We have to plan it, figure out how we are going to pay for it, where we are going to have it, who we are going to invite. (George J. J., How it all Got Started, 2012)

While Alicia picked out a gown, researched the hall options, prepared wedding announcements and looked at cakes, John's agenda for getting to the altar was much different. John was determined to do things differently this time around. Alicia was his true love and he wanted this marriage to be sealed in love, by God. His first two marriages had vows that were sealed by the state and while beautiful and special they were missing the Spirit of God that had become such an important part of his and Alicia's lives.

Making this happen would be no small feat. John and Alicia wanted to be married in the Catholic Church. Although the Church does not recognize marriages that occur outside the Catholic Church, they do require that anyone seeking marriage after divorce must go through the nullification process, a process that takes months and, in some cases, years.

"The Catholic Church presumes that marriages are valid, binding spouses for life. When couples do separate and divorce the Church examines in detail their marriage to determine if, right from the start, some essential element was missing in their relationship. If that fact has been established, it means the spouses did not have the kind of marital link that binds them together for life. The Church then issues a declaration of nullity (an annulment) and both are free to marry again in the Catholic Church."(Catholic Update, 2006-2013)

John recalls, "It was unbelievable. I had to go to the Archdiocese, fill out all kinds of paperwork, go to Ohio and Wayne County, get all the paperwork and divorce decrees, and even acquire my baptismal record. You wouldn't believe the treadmill that I was on. The reason I was willing to do all that was because this time around I wanted to do it right. I wanted to be blessed, so this is why I took all the extra steps. I wanted to straighten out some of the things that might have been my problem. So having our union blessed is a true blessing."

And so it was on September 30, 2012, that John and Alicia were wed by Father Victor Clore at Christ the King Church, right around the corner from John's home and business. Over 200 people attended the beautiful celebration of love. They gathered to share in a true joy for two people who had won their hearts. While everyone has heard of the "glowing bride," and Alicia certainly fit that part, John's own face flushed with joy and eyes glistening with emotion, touched everyone's heart. It was a joy that comes when one knows that they have tasted a piece of heaven and found a happiness that comes from the deepest depth of the soul.

The celebration that followed the ceremony was not to be beaten. Music from John's longtime friend, Eric Harris, filled the newly refurbished and reopened Community

Center. The beautiful couple were surrounded by family and friends. There was a feast fit for a king's court and libations to feed the joyous spirits. It was a night to remember. The celebration was followed by a wonderful honeymoon and a week of savoring the glorious time alone together. It was a wonderful start to a life together where the impossible would always be possible!

A week later it was back to work and the brutal routine, but John reminded everyone of his new life and the source of his great happiness every day. Posts of his beautiful bride and photos from the wedding on Facebook proclaimed his love and joy.

The man behind the curtain, the man who could evoke smoke and mirrors with a wave of his hand, had transformed.

John has been to the desert and back. He has made his way through a host of crises. And now as he faces the future, he is putting his life in order, with God at the front and Alicia by his side. An awareness fills him: "God is at the center of everything and provides meaning for our lives".

John does not need to hide behind the curtain or use illusion to communicate this message: "When we realize that our true Self is one of pure potentiality, we align with the power, that manifests everything in the universe." Understanding this potentiality, this gift of power John is positioned to accomplish great things. With the respect of the community, the foundation of a solid business, and the support of a giant network of supporters, John knows without doubt that the future is bright!

'Cuz they say two thousand zero zero party over
Oops out of time
So tonight I'm gonna party like it's 1999

I was dreamin' when I wrote this
So sue me if I go too fast

But life is just a party
and parties weren't meant to last
War is all around us
My mind says prepare to fight
So if I gotta die
I'm gonna listen to my body tonight

Yeah, they say two thousand zero zero party over
Oops out of time
So tonight I'm gonna party like it's 1999
Yeah
Prince, 1999
Prince; Party Like It's 1999;

CELEBRATION

There's a party goin' on right here
a celebration to last throughout the years
So bring your good times
and your laughter too
we're gonna celebrate
your party with you!
Come on now, celebration
Let's all celebrate and have a good time
Celebration . . .
We gonna celebrate and have a good time
It's time to come together
it's up to you
what's your pleasure
Everyone around the world
Come on . . .
Kool and the Gang; Celebration; 1980

John's idea that "life is a party" must have been inspired by his father who saw every occasion as a reason for a celebration. There were barbeques throughout the summer, where everyone from the neighborhood would casually drop in and enjoy some grilled shish-kabob with salads made by John's sisters from the vegetables grown in the family garden, followed by pinochle and other card games. Laughter and friendship were always in good measure in the George family home.

Growing up, John, like his father, took every opportunity to invite the neighborhood into his home and yard. His was the home on the block where all were welcome and all came to play, eat and create adventure. If the yard wasn't being transformed into a golf course, carnival or interactive game, the gang might be found splashing in the family pool.

Added to all of this was a love for the City. Being raised in Detroit gave John a sense of pride. Perhaps it's being one with the underdog, or maybe because something great began here and he wants to see that come to life again. Maybe the spirits of the past flow through the people who grew up here. Whatever it is, John has an unquenchable passion for the City of Detroit.

John recalls growing up: "I use to go downtown with my dad to a Tigers game, and we'd go to this place that is no longer there, the Sheik, which was a Lebanese restaurant. It had these tacky palm trees but really great food. I have a love for the City, a love for people, a love for having fun. I don't mind working really hard but I like to play hard too. I really wanted to bring people downtown to see what was going on in the City."

As John became a successful businessman with discretionary income to share, he wanted to celebrate all that life had to offer with his friends. It began in about 1983, at the Hyatt Regency Hotel a premier hotspot for young people, the ideal venue to please the partygoers. John recalls, "On the ends, there were two suites and I reserved them both. I don't know how we did it, but we basically partied on that whole end."

Each party John planned was bigger, more elaborate and outrageous than the one before it. Eric Harris, John's friend and resident DJ, became a cornerstone of each event. John had been referred to Eric to provide the entertainment at one of John's first events and he became one of John's inner circle friends. Eric had a reputation as the number one DJ of the time, with a selection of music worthy of any radio station of the day, his demeanor, edge and wildness set the mood for a crazy and memorable party every time.

Eric recalls one of the early events: "John rented a fleet of limousines, 13 or 14 of them, and we drove through the streets of downtown Detroit and around the City. It was a champagne ride with John's close friends toasting each other. John was just a wild man." (Harris, 2012)   Eric continues, "John is just a fun guy, a loving guy, a giving guy. He was just that guy who wanted to give. The party was what he wanted to give.

John's lifelong friend, Todd McKler, laughing heartily, recalls, "When we were younger, in our twenties, back in the days when we used to drink, John gave this party, at the Renaissance Center using all his own money.   He had rented the whole 69th floor, along with the 61st floor. He was using his savings to do what he wanted to. I guess he shouldn't have, but he wanted to have a party for everybody."

John himself recalls this amazing night: "I will never forget when I checked in at the front lobby.   I had two handfuls of keys, one for the 69th floor and one for the 61st floor. We had sooooooo much fun!   There have only been two other people who have rented the whole 69th floor, Prince and Ronald Regan for the Republican Convention and us! I had a half dozen ladies dressed up in black and white French maid outfits serving drinks.   We had barons of meat, all you can eat and drink."

John threw a decadent party for his friends pulling out all the stops. It was the early 80s and while the Prince song, *1999*, had not yet been written, John's event could've been the inspiration for the song.

"We just all came to the party. I mean the food, the alcohol, he did it all. They said we couldn't have a radio up there, but he had his friend, Eric Harris, DJ. John had them wrap the speakers and all the equipment in gift-wrap paper so it looked like it was gifts and took it all up there. We went around to all these stores buying the alcohol, cases and cases of alcohol, and wrapped that stuff all up. Everything went wrapped up like it was a gift and everything went upstairs. So everybody had a tux when they came there, there was music, there was dancing, there was drinking. This party must have cost him a nice penny. There must have been two hundred people. That place was packed. It was a Christmas party. It was a Christmas Party on the 69th floor! All I remember is I was walking all around that place, there were so many people. There were people everywhere. It was a party you could not forget. We partied all night long. He wanted to make this party for all his friends, everybody he knew, that was what the party was for, all his friends. Then they brought some friends and such. It was such a beautiful party. " Todd McKler

Usually the parties were planned between Christmas and New Years Eve. Friends were still in from out of town waiting for New Years Eve so it was the perfect time to throw a "mega party". "The biggest party we had," John recalls, "was a ticket event held at the Detroit Yacht Club . . . we lost count at 1555, there were well over 2000 people at that party. People were literally on the fence rocking it back and forth, "We want in, we want in! The Club was overcapacity, initiating the Wayne County Sheriff, Michigan State Police and the City of Detroit Police to show up but nobody was arrested or hurt.

John never made money at any of the events, that was never his intent, it was always to have a good time with friends, to do something out of the ordinary. John describes it: "I just love the 'Wow!' factor." A lot of people celebrating life, enjoying music, drinks and food. The mega parties were probably once a year and John hosted these events for about 6 or 7 years in a row, the Hyatt Regency Dearborn, the Renaissance Center Detroit, the Lansdown, the Roostertail, the Detroit Yacht Club, sometimes more then once at a venue. John enjoyed this time of life, sharing his successes and riches with his friends. John describes; "I used to say, if I never laughed another day in my life, I got my fair share of laughs!"

"Maybe that was a turnaround in his life. Maybe he said, '

I'm going to give up this good life and I am going to do good for others instead,' because he saw that a lot of people were hurting. He didn't have to live here. He could have left here a long time ago, but he is not leaving – he is staying right here." (McKler, 2012)

Parties have been a signature of John's life. Like his father, he believed life was to be enjoyed and that meant bringing people together to celebrate. The children's birthdays were the next opportunity for John's lavish silliness and frivolity! John William remembers his parties were exciting, filled with whatever suited his interest and, of course, the traditional clown party. Ann Marie shares, "Our birthdays were always a big deal. Dad threw me and John the best birthdays, especially me. Ponies, clowns, bounce houses, you name it, I've had it. He went all out for birthdays."

As the Blight Busters vision grew, John incorporated his parties into the business. There were parties for Angels' Night, launching new projects, and showcasing Blight Busters for media events. Eventually, Jazz Nights at Artist Village became the party venue. With hamburgers on the grill and salad fixings from the garden, it was reminiscent of the summer backyard gatherings at the Georges. John's nostalgia created a family environment for the community of Brightmore and Old Redford. People from every corner and every walk of life are drawn here because they find home, warmth and companionship that goes beyond neighbors and community; it is a place of friendship, family and love.

THE FUTURE

I think having land and not ruining it
is the most beautiful art that anybody could
ever want to own.
-Andy Warhol

So what does the future look like for John George?   John George, a walking legend who has literally crawled through what might be described as a hole to the dark side of the city, sacrificed his own personal needs, and after much blood, sweat, and tears has taken a community from bitter destitution to the doorstep of prosperity. How does one top that? Where would one go next? How about finding a nice little quiet corner of the world and taking a well-deserved break?

Hardly!   In fact, what might seem like the culmination of a dream and the realization of a master plan is only a building block for the next phase.   What is that next phase? As with the first and second phases, it has not been written down. While there are goals and a three-year strategic plan, in reality, what transpires has more to do with the resources that are made available to Blight Busters through donations, the people who will cross John's path and the plans God has for all of it. Anything is possible!

While there is no guarantee what the landscape will look like 10 or 20 years from now, one thing is certain. It will be original, eclectic, urban and a collaboration of talent and energy that is unparalleled - and whatever the plan it will be a vision shared with John's son, John William, currently the Project Manager for Blight Busters.   As John William completes his education, he is looking to preserve what his father has begun. While being open to opportunities that may come his way with a Degree in Psychology, he will certainly be doing that.

John William describes himself as the "middle ground." "My dad and Aaron (Blight Buster CFO) are like the yin and the yang. Aaron is a numbers guy and my Dad is a creative person, and I feel like I am the best of both worlds. I see where my Dad is coming from and I see where Aaron is coming from, and I am the middle ground. My dad is just a ray of sunshine, always optimistic, and that's not a bad thing. You need more people to be optimistic, but sometimes you also need someone to be realistic, one of the qualities that I feel I get from my mother."

John William's gift for being realistic contributes to his ability to organize, bring in structure and streamline processes, a real asset that will definitely have a positive impact on the future of Blight Busters. John William feels that the success of the business depends on securing funding sources. "I would like to hire more grant writers, if we were in a position to do that."

John William's realistic view includes the continuation and expansion of programs, like Collective Soul and the art programs as "icing on the cake". When examining the broad scope of the Blight Busters vision, he notes, "the cake looks nice but does it taste good?"

Looking to the future, John William proposes that projects shouldn't be started until the funding is in place. "I would like to make sure that things are all lined up like the Santa Clara 7 - the funding is in place; the employees are in place; the dumpsters are in place. Okay now let's go tear down a house." John William' decisive vision for Blight Busters will surely open doors to new projects that will launch the business into a not only profitable, but sustainable direction.

What John began as a personal mission inspired by a conviction for justice and the greater good has become a model for change. This model, a strategic plan of action for re-urbanization should have a name of it is own. Perhaps the "Warhol Effect" would be a suitable name, for this unusual collaborative approach to urban renewal.

John has elevated the concept of revitalization to a whole new level. It isn't just about taking on a block or a business district and re-energizing to draw more people into the community - although this will definitely play into the picture in the future. John's approach, not unlike Andy Warhol's is taking the ordinary and making it extraordinary. He has used what he has been given and transformed it into something that may look quite the same, but put in a new context it breathes life and calls attention. It began simply by sweeping the streets and cleaning a neighborhood and putting garbage cans out, and progressed to taking a condemned building and making it a hub for community networking. With time and further development perhaps this "Warhol Effect" may be a model to be used Citywide.

Exploring this concept, John has taken the land in Northwest Detroit and transformed it into a piece of living art. It has become not just a place for artists to convene and interact, it is much more than that, everyone from every walk of life has become the artist and the inspiration behind every garden, mural, street clean-up, and project. It is this welcoming spirit, including everyone in creating the vision, that harnesses the positive energy, that fuels the whole movement of the "Warhol Effect".

This is what attracts others to join in the effort. This is what developers saw when they choose Grand River and Six Mile to build a Meijer mega shopping center in Detroit. This is what businesses like Starbucks see when they decide to support the movement with volunteers and funds. It is this effect of seeing something old in a new dimension that captures others with vision and passion.

This form of transforming a community is referred to as an "effect" because it is dynamic and is what is taking John's vision from a project based mission to a paradigm shift in how community's of the future will be recreated into hubs where the energy and influence of the people of the community will fuel the transformation to a center that best exemplifies their distinct character while meeting their particular and unique cultural and personal needs.

Looking at the future of John can only be seen through this lens. John and his vision are bound as a mother to a child. No matter how many years pass or how mature, experienced and successful the child becomes the child will always be within the parent's thoughts and the parents within the child's thoughts, influencing each obliquely.

In the immediate future John's influence will be seen most directly through the programs and projects he has put in place. The collaboration with Michigan State University is predicted to implement financial literacy, horticulture, and educational programs within the community. A logical assumption would be that these social influences would empower the community to move beyond the obstacles they have faced in the past and be able to take control over their future to gain more stability economically and personally.

Michigan State University will also have a large impact on the development of Farm City, the urban farm that will provide the community, not just healthy food options, but employment, careers and an economic base that would provide opportunities for multi-level business investments. Self-sustaining businesses that might offer organic products created from their farms. Perhaps including clothing woven from sheep and alpaca fur to jams, jellies and preserves, along with oils, lotions, teas and personal care products crafted from local trees, plants and herbs. The sustainable farm vision would also offer an environment for agricultural education and exploration.

Meanwhile, another partner, Tech Town, will be providing the professional business strategies, creativity and entrepreneurial spirit to provide structure and direction to this ever changing and evolving urban renewal model.

All of these creative and technological influences will shape a thriving community that will become a destination for urban developers from all over the country to attend conferences and forums to educate themselves in this "Warhol" model of development. While the global economy spins its wheels in its attempt to reorganize and restructure from the financial blowout, Detroit is on the threshold of experiencing John's vision of making something out of nothing, leading the way to a promising future. John Robb, the founder of Resilient Communities, reflects that the answer to global collapse is "building resilient, dynamic local economies that thrive as the global system sputters . . . [they] have learned to produce food, energy, water, products, and incomes locally. A decentralized network like this will grow very quickly as word of their success grows.

Soon, these communities will not only replace the things that were lost with the demise of the global economy, they will find ways to improve upon them. To do better than what's possible in the current global system."

The Warhol model for urbanization could potentially lead the way for this global restructuring. Old Redford could become the center for training and be the site where these building blocks for new communities are born. This would be the next layer or phase of renewal, a center for urban development resources that would include living space for the central village as well as for guests coming into town for training. Like we have begun seeing in many retirement communities and commercial spaces, the concept of an all inclusive community would be created. Reclaiming abandoned, spaces and buildings and using reclaimed building materials the village would have a style uniquely its own. New restaurants would be built in similar fashion, serving food grown and prepared from the connecting farm. Visitors would enjoy the music, art and poetry of the village while being offered the opportunity to participate in workshops and seminars based on the "Warhol" model.

John will be the force behind this motion, the spirit that fuels the creative minds of designers and engineers. John will continue doing what he has always done, gathering the people from across the neighborhood, the city, the state, the country and the world to create "positive" change. He will be at the worksite giving direction and driving a truck to the dump; he will be in the board room advising the investors; he will be on the phone listening with compassion to the woman who is without power and food making sure that at the end of the day she is warm, comfortable and has what she needs. John will still be sporting his black Blight Busters T-shirt and ball cap with the Detroit "D" as he opens each learning session, but he will not confine himself to the classroom, John knows all too well that the real lessons to be taught and learned are on the street, and as long as he lives and breathes, that is where he will be.

A final glimpse into the future of this thriving community one should turn to be Peace Park, the nexus of hope, that will continue to be a gathering place for celebration. Peace Park will forever hold the "true treasure," the message of this Urban Warrior.

The Warhol Effect

Taking the ordinary and making it extraordinary!
Kishell

ONE TIN SOLDIER

15

Listen, children, to a story
That was written long ago,
'Bout a kingdom on a mountain
And the valley-folk below.

On the mountain was a treasure
Buried deep beneath the stone,
And the valley-people swore
They'd have it for their very own.
Go ahead and hate your neighbor,

Go ahead and cheat a friend.
Do it in the name of Heaven,
You can justify it in the end.
There won't be any trumpets blowing

Come the judgment day,
On the bloody morning after....
One tin soldier rides away.

One Tin Soldier:
The Legend of Billy Jack
Dennis Lambert & Brian Potter (1971)

Reflecting back to the question posed in the introduction: "What makes one person dedicate his life to a single vision, sacrificing personal gain in order to change so many lives?" What makes John Joseph George different from any other philanthropist or person with a cause? Just what makes him unique?

Is it his passion? Probably not, since passion fuels most people who serve others. Passion is the driving force that propels do-gooders toward their mission. Without passion, the folks who give humanity so much hope would not get very far. They would probably lose direction and enthusiasm during the early stages of forging their plan. In this regard, John, the recipient of the Michiganian of the Year Award [vi] sponsored by the Detroit News, is not unlike other recipients of the award, including such awe-inspiring people as Dr. Charles H. Wright, Berry Gordy, Jr. Rosa Parks, Dennis Archer, Dick Purtan, Ernie Harwell and John Cardinal Dearden, to name but a few.

Is it his visionary quality that makes John unique? Once again, in addition to passion, one must have vision in order to accomplish great things. Without an ability to think beyond the possible, would any person succeed in making such a difference in the world?

Could it be his humor? His son John William, describes his dad's humor, "He wants to be funny and he's just not funny. But every so often there's gems that he says that are hilarious."

Would it be his love for the City and his mission to "save the world, starting with Detroit"? Hardly, that extensive list, not only includes Kidd Rock as well as those who showed up on the TIME lists' "Committee to Save Detroit": Kym Worthy, Greg Willerer, Dan Gilbert, Doug Ross, Faye Nelson and Ismael Ahmed. There are also the pioneers who helped shaped the City from the beginning Antoine de la Mothe Cadillac, Gabrielle Richard, Chief Pontiac – and other Detroit stakeholders who profoundly changed the landscape of Detroit, such as Henry Ford, Thomas Edison, Fr. William Cunningham, and Joseph L. Hudson to name just a few.

John certainly has passion, vision, humor and a love for Detroit. There is evidence of those characteristics throughout his story. But these attributes are woven so uniquely into a suit of armor worthy of a warrior.

Of all that John is, he most embodies the presence of a warrior. And what embodies a warrior? Courage, stamina, strength, intelligence, and much more. Dr. Edward Tick author of _War and the Soul_ describes:

> "The ideal Warrior is assertive, active and energized. He or she is clear-minded, strategic, and alert. A warrior uses both body and mind in harmony and

cooperation. A warrior is disciplined. A warrior assesses both his own skills and resources and those of his opponent. A warrior is a servant of civilization and its future - guiding, protecting, and passing on information and wisdom. A warrior is devoted to causes he judges to be more important than himself or any personal relationships or gain. Having confronted death, a warrior knows how precious life is and does not abuse or profane it."

Indeed, John Joseph George is a warrior, an urban warrior, fighting for justice. Dr. Tick's description fully describes this man of vision and passion. He is truly, "servant of civilization and its future – guiding, protecting and passing on information and wisdom." Each day John leaves his home, his place of comfort and peace, to fight injustice. As any great warrior he faces each new challenge as just another step toward winning the battle. Don Juan Matus describes it this way; "The basic difference between an ordinary man and a warrior, [the] warrior takes everything as a challenge, while an ordinary man takes everything as a blessing or as a curse."

John is not just any warrior, though. He is a warrior who listen's with his soul and is guided by God - not unlike the biblical hero David, son of Jesse and slayer of Goliath.

"You come to me with sword, spear, and javelin, but I

come to you in the name of the Lord Almighty – the God of the armies of Israel, whom you have defiled. Today the Lord will conquer you . . ."

It is in this Spirit, the Spirit of God, that John fights injustice. Sometimes the beast is a "Goliath" so ominous and foreboding that it will frighten away the best of men. John however sees this beast as just another bump in the road. He perseveres with tenacity to slay the beast and move on to the next obstacle, the next naysayer, the next conundrum.

Most people, facing such a bleak and discouraging path, eventually succumb to exhaustion if not despair. Don Juan Matus ,wisdom however, sheds light on how a true warrior responds to adversity: "A warrior acknowledges his pain but he doesn't indulge in it. The mood of the warrior who enters into the unknown is not one of sadness; on the contrary, he's joyful because he feels humbled by his great fortune, confident that his spirit is impeccable, and above all, fully aware of his efficiency. A warrior's joyfulness comes from having accepted his fate, and from having truthfully assessed what lies ahead of him."

It was this purposeful acceptance that led John to leave his career in 1993 to pursue his mission of "saving the world, starting with Detroit." He made a commitment more to himself than to anyone else whether that was his family, community or civic leaders - that he was going to slay the beast of negativity and create a positive energy. It may have been about tearing down an abandoned home in the beginning but time and experience taught him that it wasn't the blight that was destroying this community. Its heart and soul were being eaten away by a giant, and it would take nothing less than a giant slayer to obliterate it. A group of people who felt abandoned by their City, who lost hope, who needed someone to be their warrior to slay the giant, found that in John George. The giant clothed in oppression, negativity, violence, hatred, and greed could only be crushed by a true warrior.

It would take a very special warrior to defeat such a giant. A "warrior of the light". This enigma of a leader and warrior is personified by author Paul Coelho in his book by the same name. "The warrior of the light has a destiny to fulfill". This "warrior of the light" is just the man that has been described so fully in these pages. Exactly when John knew this was his destiny, his spiritual calling, is hard to say. It may have been at the end of the day when he boarded up that first house and saw the drug dealers, looking on in surprise, drive away never to return. Maybe it was when he made the decision to abandon a lifestyle of comfort to pursue the Blight Busters mission. Or perhaps it was only when he identified the giant and, as a warrior, set out not to just defeat the giant, but to replace it with hope, light and a brighter tomorrow.

How does one accomplish such a feat? It takes wisdom to be sure, and the ability to discern what gifts are placed before him in the people, resources and opportunities that cross his path. This warrior is a manager of blessings. He not only discerns those blessings that are set before him but he immediately and intuitively envisions how to best integrate them into his battle plan. John greets every person he meets with enthusiasm, he listens to their story, envisions their dreams and seamlessly weaves their gifts into a plan that fortifies, enriches and builds a web of strength and confidence.

In Caelho's word, John tries "to show each person how much they are capable of achieving." In so doing he creates an army of soldiers who uphold the vision, share their own passion, talents and energy to transform the battlefield.

Such is the story of John Joseph George, the urban warrior. He is not a legend, but a real man. A man with not only a vision; but, a message. As this "one tin soldier" rides away, let us all remember his message. Peace on earth, . . . was all he said.

What makes one person dedicate his life
to a single vision, sacrificing personal
gain in order to change so many lives?

A man with a vision;
And a message.

As this "one tin soldier" rides away,

Peace on earth, . . . was all he said.

CPILOGC

The story continues . . .

As this biography was being written John continued his
work and mission. Each day John has risen to the new day,
planning the next project, taking down another torched
house, meeting community leaders to find new ways to
collaborate, meeting business leaders to develop new
partnerships and meeting with federal officials to establish
new funding opportunities.   He continues to take calls
from people who are searching for answers to their
frustrations and lack of resources while creating a strategic
plan for the future of Blight Busters. As always he works
unceasingly at fighting blight and making the impossible
possible.

So this story does not end here, instead it has a life of its
own, it is dynamic and ever changing as John's passion and
mission lead him on.

With your purchase of the Urban Warrior you are
supporting the future of Blight Busters and helping this
dream continue.   This book has been written exclusively
for the benefit of the Blight Busters Program, there were
no commission or fees associated with the writing,

publication, editing or photography - all were donated. 100% of the proceeds will return to Blight Busters to help support the good work being done to "Save the World Starting with Detroit!"

As a reader of the Urban Warrior and supporter of Blight Busters you can continue to offer your time, talent and treasure to make the impossible possible. If you would like to volunteer or make a donation please contact Blight Busters at http://www.mcbbdetroit.com ; 313-255-4355.

You, the reader, are also invited to share your story. If you would like to contribute your experience of volunteering or collaborating with the Motor City Blight Busters please email your stories to: Urban.Warrior.Kishell@gmail.com , they will be considered for the next segment of the journey to the future - to be included in a book telling the story from the perspective of the community of supporters who, none of this would be possible without.

Works Cited

Anderson, S. (2012, March 7). Steve Anderson Interview. (L. K. Huff, Interviewer)

Archer, M. D. (May). (L. K. Huff, Interviewer) Detroit, MI.

Awards Page. (1987). (S. o. Project, Producer) Retrieved from Charles Lindbergh:
http://www.charleslindbergh.com/history/moh.asp

Carter, D. (2012, July 12). Summer Mission. (L. K. Huff, Interviewer)

Chopra, D. (1993). *The Seven Spiritual Laws of Success.* (J. Mills, Ed.) Amber-Allen Publishing and New World Library.

Gallagher, M. R. *Examining the Impact of Food Deserts on Public Health in Detroit.*

Gallaher, J. *Reimaging Detroit.*

George, J. J. (2011, December 7). Angel's Night. (L. K. Huff, Interviewer)

George, J. J. (2011, December 7). Early Days Continuation. (L. K. Huff, Interviewer)

George, J. J. (2012, March 7). How it all Got Started. (L. K. Huff, Interviewer)

George, J. W. (2012, March 7). (L. K. Huff, Interviewer)

George, J. W. (2012, March 7). (L. K. Huff, Interviewer) Detroit, MIchigan.

George, V. (2012, June 13). (L. K. Huff, Interviewer)

II, P. J. (2006, April 6). *John Paul II, my favorite quotes.* Retrieved from Catholic Fire:
http://catholicfire.blogspot.com/2006/04/john-paul-ii-my-favorite-quotes.html

James Martin, S. (2010). *The Jesuit Guide to (Almost) Everything; A Spirituality for Real Life* (First ed.). Harper ONe.

John Paul II, B. S. (n.d.). Retrieved from Cathechism of the Catholic Church:
http://www.vatican.va/archive/ccc_css/archive/catechism/p4s2a3.htm#2848

Kirkland, C. (2012, July 20). (L. K. Huff, Interviewer)

Kirkland, C. A. (2012, July 18). (L. K. Huff, Interviewer)

Lexic.Us. (n.d.). Retrieved from http://www.lexic.us/definition-of/median_sternotomy

Mack, A. (2011, December 7). Albert Mack Interview. (L. K. Huff, Interviewer)

McKler, T. (2012, January 11). McKler Interview. (L. K. Huff, Interviewer)

Michigan.gov. (n.d.). *Prisoner Reentry.* Retrieved from Michigan Department of Corrections: http://michigan.gov/corrections/0,1607,7-119-9741_33218---,00.html

Mollison, B. (1988). *Permaculture: A Designers' Manual.* Tagari Publicaitons.

Mollison, B., & Tegasaste. (1988). The Permaculture Practitioner's Journal I. *The Permaculture Practitioner's Journal I* .

Silverstein, S. (1974). *Where the Sidewalk Ends.* HarperCollins.

Trembly, S. (2012, July 12). Summer Mission 2012. (L. K. Huff, Interviewer)

Trop, J. (2011, November 16). Meijer plans supercenter in Detroit at former Redford High site. *The Detroit News* .

About the Cover Photographer

Cover photos courtesy of Dave Budnick.

Dave is a freelance photographer based in the Metropolitan Detroit area specializing in weddings, corporate photography and portraits. His intrigue with cameras began when he purchased a new camera to take photos at the end of Navy boot camp. What began as a desire to photograph all the places he would travel to around the world became more than just a hobby when he was appointed as the submarine's photographer. His love for photography grew through the years as technology changed and he continued to upgrade and hone his skills. From photographing friends and family to capture those treasured moments Dave has turned his passion into a professional business. Dave is a long time supporter of the Motor City Blight Busters and has volunteered many hours through the years. To view his personal and professional work or arrange for a photo session visit www.davebudnick.com.

About the Editor

Editing courtesy of
Faith Doody

Faith grew up in Redford
Township, Michigan, and
married a boy from the
Brightmoor District. Like Lynne Kishel Huff and
John George, she is a proud alumnus of Bishop
Borgess High School. She graduated from the
University of Detroit and has worked as a high
school English teacher; a proofreader, editor and
copywriter; and a coordinator of middle school faith
formation. Her greatest work in progress is raising
five sons with her husband Gary. She has been
privileged to work side-by-side with the Motor City
Blight Busters and the youth of Christ the
Redeemer during Spring and Summer Missions for
the past nine years, with many more to come. She
feels profoundly blessed to play even the tiniest role
in this incredible story.

John William George, Kishell and John George

About the Author

Kishell, Lynne Huff Kishel, has been an artist of the pen and ink for many years, beginning at just ten years old she spent her summers writing stories for family and friends. As an adult her love for written word led her to freelance write for local newspapers which was followed by publishing her first book, *Thank You For All You've Done for Me*, in 2008. (Lynne Kishel Huff) The book is written with the parents of teenagers in mind and offers research and resources to create a time of celebration during the teen years. Available through Amazon.com.

Along with writing Kishell has spent over half of her life in a career advocating for youth, teaching the importance of giving to others and answering the call to justice.

As a Youth Minister she led teens to discover the joy of giving to others. In the late 1990's her Summer Mission program, took teens to the City of Detroit to work with the Motor City Blight Busters. While the teens enjoyed tearing down the abandoned houses, they also learned about oppression and planting seeds of justice. Through the years they assisted in many projects including, gutting the structure that has transformed into the Java House, cleaning the streets of Old Redford, tearing down and building up, constructing and planting a Peace Pole in Peace Park, creating flower and vegetable gardens, and most of all building friendships that continue to this day. They learned creating justice is about community and making friends - that changing an environment will bring peace and compassion, that transforming injustice brings justice.

During these years Kishell's friendship with John George grew and they found they had the same vision and passion for changing the face of Detroit and bringing hope to these people of goodwill. As the manuscript, Urban Warrior, began to take shape, Kishell continued her passion of "making a difference" leading a Statewide service learning initiative, part of Global Youth Service Day, bringing together over 2,500 teens and hundreds of adults to volunteer in service projects throughout Michigan.

Kishell's own passion to make the impossible possible has filled her life. Urban Warrior brings a lifetime goal to fruition and it is her hope to instill in others the same desire to reach out and "make an extraordinary difference one heart of hope at a time - one hand at a time.

Kishell's blog, www.xtraordinarydifference.com embraces this message offering stories of making the extraordinary difference. Readers enjoy a variety of outreach experiences, while inviting them to share their own stories, ideas and resources in hopes to inspire others to Make the Xtra Ordinary Difference!

**Make an extraordinary difference
one heart of hope at a time
one hand at a time.**

www.xtraordinarydifference.com

Other Books by Kishell

Thank You For All You've Done for Me;
Lynne Kishel Huff

Books to be Released

Fiction

Diamonds R 4ever

Non-Fiction

Urban Warrior the Compendium

Inspirational

Journey to Tomorrow

---

[i] Anniversary Souvenir, CH Krugler & Company p. 21

[ii] Physically, St. Elmo's fire is a bright blue or violet glow, appearing like fire in some circumstances, from tall, sharply pointed structures such as lightning rods, masts, spires and chimneys, and on aircraft wings. St. Elmo's fire can also appear on leaves, grass, and even at the tips of cattle horns. Often accompanying the glow is a distinct hissing or buzzing sound. It is sometimes confused with ball lightning.

Conditions that can generate St.Elmo's fire are present during thunderstorms, when high voltage levels are present between clouds and the ground underneath. Air molecules glow due to the effects of such voltage, producing St. Elmo's fire.

[iii] *Networking our Vision of the Core Concepts of Art;* by Ludwig Tuman; Excerpt

from essay for 1999 Bahá'í Conference on Social & Economic Development; Orlando, Florida

[iv] "The development of the Brightmoor community is a product of the enormous demand for housing in Detroit corresponding to the growth of the automobile industry. It is one of the first of its kind in the country, beginning as a business investment by an innovative real estate developer, B. E. Taylor, who understood the powerful desire for home ownership. Taylor depended on the economic conditions of Detroit, creative marketing strategies, and an aesthetically pleasing design. Most importantly, the success of Taylor's Brightmoor subdivisions as desirable places to live depended on the cooperation of its residents in building and maintaining a community. However, because of unsanitary living conditions and the unanticipated economic collapse in the 1930s, Brightmoor did not live up to Taylor's vision." Final Report: Proposed B.E. Taylor's Subdivision House Historic District 15378 Lamphere, Brightmoor; the Detroit City Council; Historic Designation Advisory Board, accordance with Chapter 25 of the 1984 Detroit City Code and the Michigan Local Historic Districts Act. October 28, 2008

[vivi] *"Every year since 1978, readers of The Detroit News have participated in nominating our Michiganians of the Year, a selection of outstanding citizens who have helped make living in this state a richer experience for the rest of us, either by their good works or by the example they set."*

From The Detroit News:
http://www.detroitnews.com/article/99999999/SPECIAL02/106020302#ix
zz1sVZBxPTT

Permissions
All manuscript photographs were obtained from the personal collections of author and John George with permission.
Cover photos were authorized for use by Photographer, Dave Budnick

All interviewees gave permission and were given full knowledge that portions of their interview would be included in Urban Warrior.